RHONA SNELLING

SPEAK YOUR MIND

STUDENT'S BOOK
+ access to Student's App and Digital Workbook

S
STARTER

macmillan education

	Outcomes	Vocabulary	Grammar	Speaking
Unit 1 Me pp. 5–13	• Introduce yourself • Talk about your nationality and language • Share information about your family	• Introductions and greetings • Countries and nationalities • Family	• *be* statements • Subject pronouns and *be* statements • *yes/no* questions with *be* Grammar Reference pp. 70–71	• Make introductions • Give personal information • Ask questions about a partner's family
	Language and Life—Communication: Personal Information			
Unit 2 My Place pp. 15–23	• Introduce your partner • Talk about classroom objects • Talk about where things are in a room	• Describing places • Your things • Prepositions of place 1	• *be* information questions • *a/an* singular and plural nouns • *There is / There are* Grammar Reference pp. 71–73	• Describe a person • Talk about your classroom • Describe a room
	Language and Life—Communication: Hotel Room			
Unit 3 Life and Work pp. 25–33	• Share information about people in your class • Ask and answer questions • Talk about how often you do things	• Jobs • Prepositions of time • Daily activities	• Simple present statements • *yes/no* questions with simple present • Adverbs of frequency Grammar Reference pp. 73–74	• Talk about a partner's life • Ask a partner *yes/no* questions • Discuss routines
	Language and Life—Communication: Meet Someone			
Unit 4 My City pp. 35–43	• Ask and answer questions about a tour • Ask for and give directions • Talk about your clothes	• Places in a city • Prepositions of place 2 • Clothes	• Simple present information questions • Imperatives • *this/that/these/those* Grammar Reference pp. 74–76	• Ask and answer questions about a tour • Ask for and give directions • Describe clothes
	Language and Life—Communication: Shop			
Unit 5 Free Time pp. 45–53	• Talk about what you can/can't do • Talk about objects in a classroom • Discuss the weather in different places	• Free-time activities • Subjects • Types of weather	• *can/can't* • Possessive *'s* • Present progressive statements Grammar Reference pp. 76–78	• Find out about free-time activities people in the class can/can't do • Talk about people's possessions • Tell a partner what you are doing / not doing
	Language and Life—Communication: Your City			
Unit 6 Health pp. 55–63	• Describe people's appearance • Talk about food and meals • Ask and answer a quiz	• The face and body • Food • Feelings	• *have* • *some* and *any* • Review Grammar Reference pp. 78–79	• Describe someone to a partner • Plan a meal with a partner • Complete a class quiz
	Language and Life—Communication: Cafe			

Confident Communicator	Pronunciation	Listening/Reading	Thinking Skills	Writing
Start Talking • Join a conversation *Repair It* • Correct yourself *Keep Talking* • Ask questions	• Word stress	Listen to a short conversation with an introduction • Skill—Listen for names Read a selection of ID cards • Skill—Locate information in a text Listen to a short conversation about a family • Skill—Understand key words	• Evaluate • Analyze	An introduction
Unit Review p. 14 **Study Skills**—Using a Dictionary				
Keep Talking • Give extra information *Keep Talking* • Ask questions *Keep Talking* • Check you understand	• Plural nouns	Listen to an interview • Skill—Use visuals to predict content Listen to a radio show • Skill—Listen for main idea Read a college webpage • Skill—Identify the topic	• Analyze • Evaluate • Brainstorm	A text message
Unit Review p. 24 **Follow A Pro**—Online Teacher				
Repair It • Ask questions *Keep Talking* • Check you understand *Keep Talking* • Useful phrases	• Word stress in questions	Read a magazine article about jobs • Skill—Scan for jobs Listen to a job interview • Skill—Listen for names, dates and numbers Read an online article about a hotel • Skill—Recognize different text types	• Evaluate • Analyze	A post
Unit Review p. 34 **Study Skills**—Recording Vocabulary				
Keep Talking • Take turns *Keep Talking* • Finish a conversation *Repair It* • Useful phrases	• Vowel sounds 1	Read an informative text • Skill—Locate information in a text Listen to a short conversation with directions • Skill—Understand key words Listen to people's shopping routines • Skill—Identify information	• Analyze • Evaluate	A description
Unit Review p. 44 **Follow A Pro**—Tour Guide				
Keep Talking • Explain your answer *Keep Talking* • Useful phrases *Keep Talking* • Show understanding	• Stress in *can/ can't*	Listen to a college radio show • Skill—Listen for main idea Read a college webpage • Skill—Scan for key words Listen to a group video call • Skill—Listen for reasons	• Analyze • Recall • Brainstorm	A blog
Unit Review p. 54 **Study Skills**—Practicing Vocabulary				
Keep Talking • Think about your answer *Keep Talking* • Useful phrases *Keep Talking* • Ask follow-up questions	• Vowel sounds	Listen to two conversations describing people • Skill—Identify information Read two different types of text • Skill—Recognize different text types Listen to a radio interview • Skill—Identify information in an introduction	• Analyze • Evaluate • Predict	An online review
Unit Review p. 64 **Follow A Pro**—Food Scientist				

The alphabet

0.01 Listen to the letters of the alphabet.

A	B	C	D	E	F	G
H	I	J	K	L	M	N
O	P	Q	R	S	T	U
	V	W	X	Y	Z	

Numbers

0.02 Listen to the numbers 1–20.

1 one	8 eight	15 fifteen
2 two	9 nine	16 sixteen
3 three	10 ten	17 seventeen
4 four	11 eleven	18 eighteen
5 five	12 twelve	19 nineteen
6 six	13 thirteen	20 twenty
7 seven	14 fourteen	21 twenty-one

Months, dates, days

January | February | March | April | May | June
July | August | September | October
November | December

JANUARY

MONDAY	TUESDAY	WEDNESDAY	THURSDAY	FRIDAY	SATURDAY	SUNDAY
1	2	3	4	5	6	7
8	9	10	11	12	13	14
15	16	17	18	19	20	21
22	23	24	25	26	27	28
29	30	31				

January 1, 2020
March 5, 2020
August 22, 2020

Times

six o'clock

six-thirty

a.m.

p.m.

Prices

change

one dollar

five dollars

ten dollars

one hundred dollars

two hundred dollars

Colors

red

yellow

blue

green

orange

purple

black

white

UNIT 1 Me

WHAT DO YOU ALREADY KNOW?

1 Think about letters and numbers. Complete the boxes.

2 IN PAIRS Share and compare your words. Add your partner's information to the boxes, if possible.

Your name: ______________________

Your partner's name: ______________________

Your cell number: ______________________

Your partner's cell number: ______________________

Your house number or name: ______________________

Your partner's house number or name: ______________________

DISCUSS & SHARE

VIDEO

3 IN GROUPS Watch the video and answer the question.

SYM Numbers or words?

In this unit, you will ...

- introduce yourself to your group, talk about your nationality and language and share information about your family.
- use thinking skills: evaluate and analyze.
- read a variety of ID cards for information.
- use strategies to start a conversation, use language to repair mistakes while talking and ask extra questions to continue a conversation.
- use communication skills to complete a form and write an introduction.
- learn skills to identify parts of a dictionary definition.

Introductions

VOCABULARY introductions and greetings

A **Match the pictures with the people.**

co-workers friends teacher and student

1 
______

2 
______

3 
______

B 1.01 **Read and listen. Match the conversations (1–3) with the pictures from A. Write the number.**

Conversation 1 ______
A: **Good morning,** Sara. **How are you?**
B: **Hi,** Mr. Webster. **I'm fine, thanks.**

Conversation 2 ______
A: **Good afternoon,** I'm Mr. Smith. What's your name?
B: My name's Nick. Nice to meet you, Mr. Smith.
A: **Nice to meet you, too.**

Conversation 3 ______
A: Good night, Lara.
B: Good night. **See you,** Mia!
A: Goodbye.

C **Add the bold phrases from B to the table.**

Say hello	Meet friends	Meet new people	Say bye
Hello	How are you?	Nice to meet you.	Goodbye.
Good morning,	**3**	**4**	Good night.
1			**5**
2			

MAKE IT REAL

My name's Nicole. = I'm Nicole.

D IN PAIRS **Practice the conversations in B.**

LISTENING

A 1.02 **Listen to the conversation. How many people talk: two, three or four?**

B 1.02 LISTENING SKILL—Listen for names **Listen again. Write the correct names.**

Maria Mr. Taylor Pedro

The man's name is ______________ .

The woman's name is ______________ .

C 1.02 THINKING SKILL—Evaluate **Listen again. Are Maria and Peter students or co-workers?**

GRAMMAR *be statements*

A **Look at the sentences below. The verb *to be* is underlined. Circle the negative (-) sentence.**

My name <u>isn't</u> Emma. My name<u>'s</u> Eva.

B **Complete the table with *isn't* and *'s*.**

Possessive Adjectives (Subject)		*To be* Affirmative	*To be* Negative	Object
My	name	is / ________	is not / ________	Emma.
Your				
His/Her				

C **Choose the correct words to complete the rules.**

1. The sentence order is **subject–verb–object** / **verb–subject–object**.
2. The apostrophe (') substitutes a **letter** / **word**, e.g., name is = name's, is not = isn't.

For more practice, go to page 70.

D 1.03 **Complete the conversation. Then listen and check your answers.**

Rosie: Hello, I'm Rosie. What's your name?
Eva: Hi, Rosie. My *name's* Eva.
Rosie: Nice to meet you, Emma.
Eva: No. My name ________ Emma. ________ name's Eva. This is my co-worker, Roger.
Rosie: Nice to meet you, Robert.
Eva: No. His name isn't Robert. ________ name ________ Roger.

E **IN GROUPS Take turns to practice the conversation. Use your own names.**

SPEAKING

A **IN GROUPS Take turns to say hello and meet your group.**

A: Hello, what's your name?
B: I'm Irene. Nice to meet you!

A: Hi, Sophie, how are you?
B: I'm fine, thanks.

B **Join another group or work as a class. Say hello and meet everyone in your group/class. Use the Confident Communicator box to help you.**

CONFIDENT COMMUNICATOR
START TALKING

To join a conversation, use the following phrases:
Excuse me, can I join you?
Hi there, can I join you?

READING

A 1.04 **Read the cards (1–4) and match them to the different types (a–d). Write the number.**

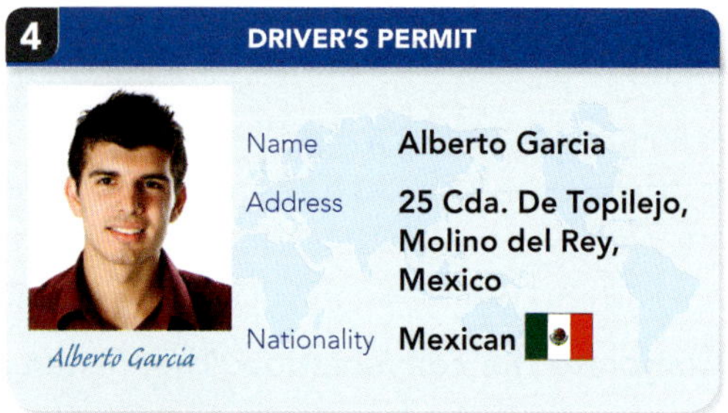

a business card ______

b driver's license ______

c online profile ______

d student ID card ______

B **READING SKILL—Locate information in a text** **Read the cards in A again and circle the names of countries. Then underline the nationalities and languages.**

C **Read again. Complete the sentences with countries, nationalities or languages.**

1 Mike is from the ____________ . He's American. His first language is English.
2 Alberto and Tino are from Mexico. They're ____________ .
3 Jane is from Great Britain. She's ____________ .

D **THINKING SKILL—Analyze** **What does *first language* mean? What is your first language?**

VOCABULARY countries and nationalities

A **Complete the table with words from READING A and your dictionary.**

Name	Country	Nationality	Language
Mike	the **1**	American	English, German, **7**
Alberto	Mexico	Mexican	Spanish
Tino	Mexico	Mexican	Spanish, English, **8** , **9**
Jane	the UK	**3**	English, French
	Canada	**4**	
	Brazil	**5**	
	2	Chinese	
	Germany	**6**	

MAKE IT YOURS

IN PAIRS Add more country and nationality words.

PRONUNCIATION word stress

A 1.05 **Listen to the words. Underline the stressed syllable.**

1 o O o o A-me-ri-can
2 O o o Me-xi-can
3 o o O Ja-pa-nese
4 O o Spa-nish
5 o O Chi-nese

B 1.06 **Listen to the words. Write the number of the correct syllable pattern group from A. Not all groups are used.**

1 Brazilian ______
2 British ______
3 Canadian ______
4 English ______
5 German ______

C 1.07 **Listen and check your answers in B. Then listen again and repeat.**

GRAMMAR subject pronouns and *be* statements

A Read the texts from READING A and choose the correct answers.

1 Mike is / isn't from China. He's / isn't from the US.
2 Tino and Alberto are / aren't from Mexico. They're / They aren't Mexican.
3 Jane is / isn't from the US. She's / isn't from Britain.

B Complete the table with *'s, isn't, 're* and *aren't*.

Subject Pronouns	*To be* Affirmative	*To be* Negative	Language
I	am / 'm	am not / 'm not	American. / from the US.
You	are / 're	are not / aren't	
He/She	is / ______	is not / ______	
We/They	are / ______	are not / ______	

For more practice, go to page 70.

C Complete the sentences with the correct form of *to be*.

1 I'm American. I __'m__ from New York City.
2 We ______ from China. We're from Brazil.
3 You aren't Canadian. You ______ from the US.
4 He ______ German. He isn't from Japan.

SPEAKING

A Complete the ID card to make it true for you.

Name: ______
Address: ______
Nationality: ______
First language: ______
Other languages: ______

CONFIDENT COMMUNICATOR
REPAIR IT

To repair your conversation after a mistake, say *Excuse me / Sorry.*
He's from Mexico. **Excuse me.**
She's from Mexico.

B IN PAIRS Show your ID card. Take turns giving information. Include one negative sentence. Use the Confident Communicator box to help you.

I'm Gabriela Marino. I'm from Mexico. I'm not from Brazil.

C Join another pair. Introduce your partner.

She's Gabriela Marino. She's from Mexico. She isn't from Brazil.

VOCABULARY family

A Look at the pictures. Complete the description with the correct names.

Owen 18, Dan 21,
Vicky 15

Joe 48, Nora 42,
my ____________

Adam 77, Vivian 73,
my ____________

I'm Owen. Dan is my **brother** and ________ is my **sister**. My parents are Joe and Nora. ________ is my **father** and Nora is my **mother**. They're **husband** and **wife**. My **grandparents** are ________ and Vivian. Adam is my **grandfather** and ________ is my **grandmother**. They're husband and wife, too.

B Complete the table with words from A.

brother	**3** ____________	parents
1 ____________	mother	grandparents
husband	**4** ____________	
2 ____________	grandmother	
son	daughter	

MAKE IT REAL

We use short words for our own parents: *father* = *dad*, *mother* = *mom*. In British English, people say *mum*.

C 1.08 Listen and check your answers to B. Then listen again and repeat.

LISTENING

A 1.09 THINKING SKILL—Evaluate Listen to the conversation. Are the speakers friends or family? Decide and give reasons.

B 1.09 LISTENING SKILL—Understand key words Listen again. Circle the answer.

1 Zoe is Ben's sister / friend.
2 Max is Ben's friend / brother.
3 Hannah and Gavin are Ben's co-workers / classmates.
4 Ben's grandparents are over 70 / 80 years old.

GRAMMAR *yes/no* questions with *be*

A Match the questions (1–4) to the answers (a–d) from LISTENING B.

1 Are they your grandparents? ________
2 Is he your brother? ________
3 Are they your classmates? ________
4 Is she your sister? ________

a No, he isn't.
b Yes, she is.
c No, they aren't.
d Yes, they are.

B Complete the table with the correct verb forms.

Question			Answer		
To be	Pronoun	Object	*Yes/no*	Pronoun	*To be*
1	she	your sister?	Yes,	he/she	**3**
	he	your father?	No,		isn't.
2	they	your grandparents?	Yes,	they	are.
			No,		**4**
Are	you	his brother?	Yes,	I	am.
			No,		am (I'm) not.

C Look at the table and complete the rules.

To make a question:
1 Put the verb *to be* at the **beginning** / **end**.
2 Put the pronoun **before** / **after** the verb *to be*.

To make an answer:
3 **Use** / **Do not use** the pronoun from the question.
4 Put the verb *to be* at the **beginning** / **end**.

For more practice, go to page 71.

D Choose the correct words.

1 (Is) / Are he your brother? No, he isn't.
2 Are they your parents? Yes, they **are** / **is**.
3 Is she your classmate? No, she **is** / **isn't**.
4 Are they your co-workers? Yes, **he are** / **they are**.
5 Is **he** / **she** your friend? Yes, she is.

SPEAKING

A Think of five friends or people in your family. Write their names and their ages.

Sonia 30

B IN GROUPS Ask questions about the people your group member chose in A. Give short answers. Use the Confident Communicator box to help you.

A: Is Sonia your sister? *B: No, she isn't.*
A: Is she your friend? *B: No, she isn't.*
A: Is she your co-worker? *B: Yes, she is!*

CONFIDENT COMMUNICATOR
KEEP TALKING

To continue a conversation, ask extra questions.
Is Pierre French? *No, he isn't.*
OK, is he from Brazil? *Yes, he is.*

C Share information about the people with the class.

Sonia is Ana's co-worker. She's 30.

Language and Life

Communication – Personal Information

FUNCTIONAL LANGUAGE complete a form

A 1.10 **Listen to the conversation and choose the correct place.**

1

Hospital

2

Hotel

3

School

B 1.11 **Read and listen to the rest of the conversation. Put the information in the correct order.**

Major ______ Email ________________ Name *1* Nationality ______ Phone number ____________

Mrs. Jones: So, your name is Rodrigo. What's your last name?
Rodrigo: My last name is Casal.
Mrs. Jones: Sorry. Can you repeat that, please?
Rodrigo: Casal. C-a-s-a-l.
Mrs. Jones: Thanks. Are you from Colombia?
Rodrigo: Yes, I am. I'm from Bogotá. I'm Colombian.
Mrs. Jones: What's your major? Is it English?
Rodrigo: My majors are English and Business.
Mrs. Jones: Great. Thanks. What's your email?
Rodrigo: My email is rodrigo1234@funmail.cg.
Mrs. Jones: And what's your phone number?
Rodrigo: My cell is (555) 555-1058.
Mrs. Jones: Thank you, Rodrigo. Welcome to college!

C 1.11 **Listen again and circle the correct answers to complete Rodrigo's form.**

Name	*Rodrigo Casal / Rodrigo Casel*
Nationality	*Colombia / Colombian*
Major	*English / English and Business*
Email	*rodrigoc1234 / rodrigo1234@funmail.cg*
Phone number	*(216) 555-1058 / (555) 555-1058*

D **IN PAIRS** **Practice the conversation in B. Switch roles.**

E **IN NEW PAIRS** **Take turns to practice the conversation in B again and give answers for you. Make notes on your partner's answers.**

WRITING an introduction

A Look at the bold letters and circle them.

capital letter

I'm from **M**exico.

B Circle the capital letters in the introduction.

Home | Classes | Students | Jobs | Contact us

LEARN **ENGLISH**

LEARN ENGLISH > FORUM > INTRODUCTIONS

Hello! My name is Rodrigo. I'm Mexican. My first language is Spanish. I also speak English and Chinese.

1 day ago

C Cross out the incorrect writing rule.

Use a capital letter for the:

- *first letter in a sentence*
- *first letter in someone's name*
- *language*
- *nationality*
- *pronoun I*
- *verb*

D Find and correct the errors in each sentence.

1. hello, i'm henry. ____________________
2. i'm from Great Britain. ____________________
3. my first Language is english. ____________________

E Rewrite the sentences in D with your personal information.

____

____

____

____

____

F IN PAIRS Exchange sentences. Check that your partner uses capital letters and periods.

MAKE IT DIGITAL

Find and take a free English class online.

VOCABULARY review

SCORE: / 5

A Complete the sentences with the words from the box.

Canadian good mother nice wife

1 A: ________ morning, my name's Dan.
B: ________ to meet you, Dan. I'm Tara.

2 Here are my parents: Nigel is my father and Karen's my ________ . They are from Canada.
They're ________ .

3 A: I'm Sam. This is my husband, Nico.
B: I'm Nico. This is my ________ , Samantha.

GRAMMAR review

SCORE: / 5

A Complete the sentences with the correct form of *be*.

1 **A:** My name ________ Nina. What's your name?
B: I ________ Suzy.

2 Carmen and Miguel are from Spain. They ________ from Great Britain.

3 **A:** ________ he your brother?
B: No, he ________ . He's my friend.

6–10 correct: You can use greetings, introduce yourself, talk about countries and nationalities, give personal information, and talk about your family. You can use *be* statements, subject pronouns and *yes/no* questions with *be*.
0–5 correct: Look again at the Vocabulary and Grammar sections in the unit.

TOTAL SCORE: / 10

WHAT DO YOU KNOW NOW? Look back at the unit and review the language you know now.

STUDY SKILLS USING A DICTIONARY

A IN PAIRS Is your dictionary a book or online? Show it to your partner. Is it the same dictionary?

B Number the explanations of the parts of the dictionary entry from www.macmillandictionary.com.

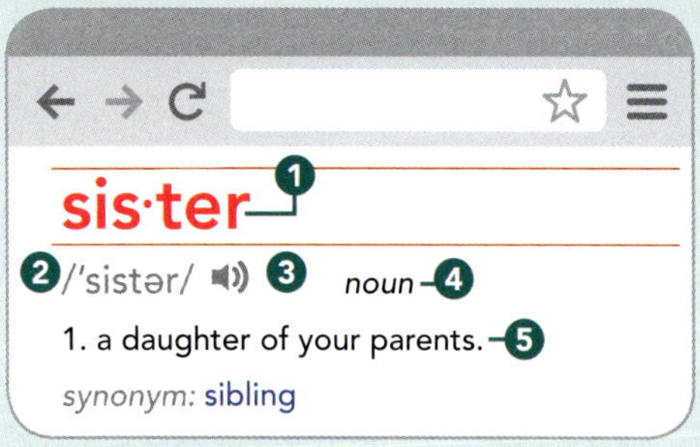

definition ____
part of speech ____
the word ____
pronunciation 1— the phonetics ____
pronunciation 2— listen to the word ____

C Answer the questions.

1 Is *sister* an adjective? ________________
2 *Sister* is for a female. What is the male word? ________________
3 How many syllables are there in *sister*? ________________
4 Which syllable is stressed? ________________

D IN PAIRS Find the words for Student A or Student B in the Macmillan Dictionary. Tell your partner the definition, correct pronunciation and part of speech. Use the word in a sentence.

Student A: bedroom, cousin Student B: garage, uncle

UNIT 2 My Place

WHAT DO YOU ALREADY KNOW?

1 Think about rooms in your home. Write words that you know in the box.

2 **IN PAIRS** Share and compare your information. Add more words to the box, if possible.

Living room: *sofa,* ____________________

____

____

Bedroom: *bed,* ____________________

____

____

Kitchen: *oven,* ____________________

____

____

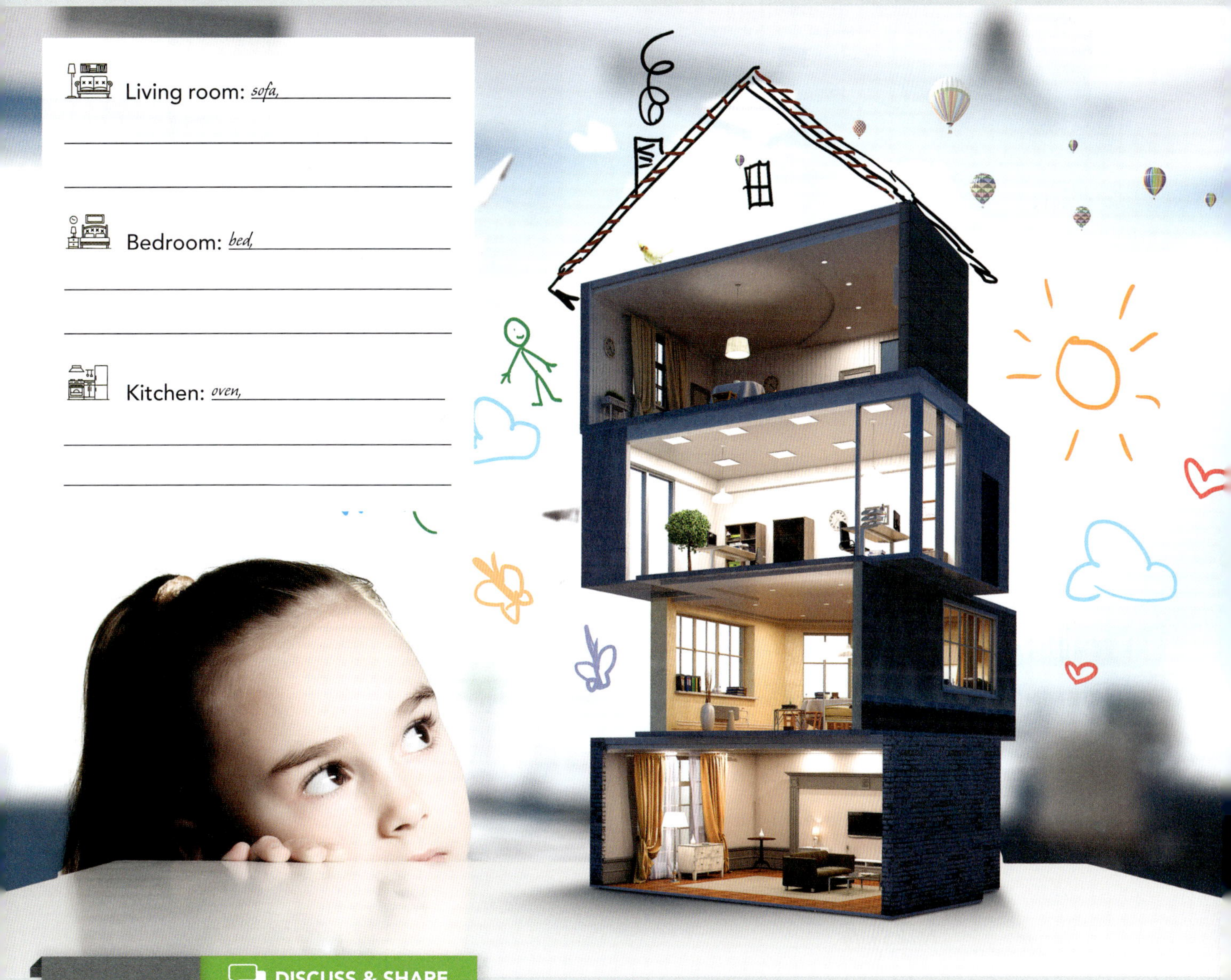

DISCUSS & SHARE

VIDEO

3 **IN GROUPS** Watch the video and answer the question.

SYM City or country?

In this unit, you will ...

- introduce your partner, talk about classroom objects and talk about where items are in a room.
- use thinking skills: analyze, evaluate and brainstorm.
- read about college student rooms.
- use strategies to give extra information and ask about new words to continue a conversation and check understanding.
- use communication skills to book a hotel room and write a text message.
- follow an online teacher to learn about their job and the skills needed to be in this industry.

VOCABULARY describing places

A **IN PAIRS** Match the adjectives from the box to the pictures. Which home is your favorite?

beautiful big modern noisy old quiet small ugly

1

____

2

____

B Look at the adjectives in A again. Find pairs with opposite meanings.

beautiful–ugly ______________________________

C 2.01 Listen and repeat.

D **IN PAIRS** Answer the question. Which adjectives describe your home?

MAKE IT YOURS

Write more adjectives to describe your home. Use your dictionary to help you.

LISTENING

A **LISTENING SKILL—Use visuals to predict content** Look at the picture. Who are the people? Where are they? What is the conversation about?

B 2.02 Listen and check your ideas from A.

C 2.02 Listen again. Complete the notes about Nick.

Name	*Nick Smith*
Home	*London—big and* ____________ *apartment (on vacation with his* ____________*)*
Age	____________
Email	____________*@gomail.com*

D **THINKING SKILL—Analyze** Juno says his place is *small* and *noisy*. Do you think he likes it or not?

GRAMMAR *be information questions*

A Complete the questions from the conversation.

how how old what ×2 where who

1 ___________'s your name?
2 ___________ are you?
3 ___________ are you from?
4 ___________ is he?
5 ___________ are you?
6 ___________'s your phone number?

B Circle the verbs in the questions in A.

C Complete the table with *is* or *are*.

Question Word	*To be*	Subject
How old	1 *are*	your parents?
What	2	your email?
Where	3	they from?
Who	4	she?
How	5	you?

D Read the questions in A and C. Match the question words (1–4) to the information in the answer (a–d). Write the letter.

1 How old ____
2 What ____
3 Where ____
4 Who ____

a a thing or a number
b a place
c a person or people
d age

For more practice, go to page 71.

E Find and correct the errors in the questions.

1 ~~What~~ *How* old is your apartment? It's 100 years old.
2 How is his email? It's benji123@yes.co.uk.
3 Where are their names? Sasha and Tina.
4 Who is she from? She's from Canada.
5 What are they? They're my friends.

F IN PAIRS Ask and answer the questions in A so they're true for you.

SPEAKING

A IN PAIRS Role-play. Read the information. Take turns to ask and answer questions. Write the answers in your notebook. Use the Confident Communicator box to help you.

Student A: go to page 65 of the Activity Bank. Student B: go to page 66 of the Activity Bank.

B Ask the questions again and answer with true information for you.

C IN GROUPS Tell the group about your partner.

A: His/Her name is …
B: He's/She's from … His/Her apartment/house is …
A: He's/She's … years old.
B: His/Her phone number is …

CONFIDENT COMMUNICATOR
KEEP TALKING

To continue the conversation, give extra information in your answer:
I'm from London.
It's a beautiful city.

VOCABULARY your things

A Look at the objects in the pictures. Check (✓) the objects you see in your classroom.

1  ☐ ____________

2  ☐ ____________

3  ☐ ____________

4  ☐ ____________

5  ☐ ____________

6  ☐ ____________

7  ☐ ____________

8 

☐ ____________

9  ☐ ____________

10 

☐ ____________

B **IN PAIRS** Match the words from the box to the pictures. Write the words in A.

brush	ID card	laptop	notebook	pen
phone	transit card	umbrella	wallet	watch

C 2.03 Listen and check your answers in B. Then listen again and repeat.

LISTENING

A 2.04 **LISTENING SKILL—Listen for main idea** Listen and discuss. Where are the people?

at a sports event in a class on a radio program

B 2.04 Listen again. Write the name of the person from the box.

Andrea Emily Ryan

1 British ____________ 2 German ____________ 3 the winner ____________

C 2.04 Listen again and complete the lists for each person. Then write the total number of items.

1 Andrea: a ____________ , 2 watches, a sandwich
Total = ____________

2 Emily: 2 brushes, an ____________ , a notebook, 2 pens, a ____________ , an umbrella, a transit card
Total = ____________

3 Ryan: 2 ID cards, a ____________ , 3 pens, a phone, a wallet, a ____________ , a transit card
Total = ____________

MAKE IT YOURS

Say *Congratulations!* or *Good job!* to a competition winner or someone with good news, e.g., a good test result.

D **THINKING SKILL—Evaluate** Are radio shows popular in your country? Describe your favorite radio show/station or your favorite radio show host.

GRAMMAR *a/an* singular and plural nouns

A Look at the bold and underlined nouns in LISTENING C and answer the questions.

1 Are the bold nouns singular (one item) or plural (2+ items)? The underlined nouns? __________ __________
2 What words are before the bold nouns? __________ __________
3 What is the final letter of each underlined noun? __________

B Complete the rules with your answers from A.

For one item, use:
1 _____ + noun, e.g., a *brush*
2 _____ + noun beginning with a vowel sound (*a, e, i, o, u*), e.g., *an umbrella*

For two or more items, use:
number + noun + **3** _____, e.g., 2 pens
number + noun ending with *–ch* and *–sh* + **4** _____, e.g., 2 watches

For more practice, go to page 72.

C Look at the items in LISTENING C again. Add more examples using the rules in B.

1 a brush, __________
2 an umbrella, __________
3 2 pens, __________
4 2 watches, __________

D Complete the lists with *a, an, –s* or *–es*.

Harry: a laptop, three watch _____, __________ pen, two notebook _____, two sandwich _____

Beth: two brush _____, __________ bag, __________ umbrella, __________ ID card, three pen _____

E IN GROUPS Choose one person from D or LISTENING C and take turns to read his or her list of things.

PRONUNCIATION plural nouns

A 2.05 Listen to the words and the final *–s* sound. Repeat.

/s/	/z/	/ɪz/
laptops	phones	watches
1	**3**	**5**
2	**4**	**6**

B 2.06 Listen and add the words to the table in A. Then listen again, check and repeat.

brushes ID cards notebooks sandwiches umbrellas wallets

SPEAKING

A IN PAIRS Make a list of things you see in the classroom, on your desk or in your bags. Use your dictionary for new words.

6 bags, 5 phones ...

B Discuss your list with another pair. Use the Confident Communicator box to help you. Is the use of *a/an* and *–s/–es* correct?

C What is the total number of things on your list? Discuss as a class.

CONFIDENT COMMUNICATOR
KEEP TALKING

To continue the conversation, ask questions about new words:
What's this in English? It's a tablet.
What's ... in English? Sunglasses.

VOCABULARY prepositions of place 1

A Look at the pictures. Complete the phrases with the words from the box.

bag | bed | chair | desk | door | umbrella | watch | window

1 in the ______

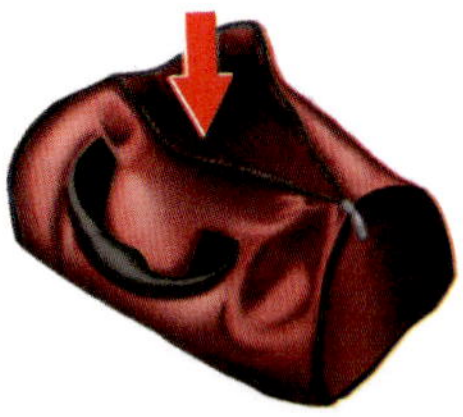

2 behind the ______

3 in front of the ______

4 between the ______ and the ______

5 next to the ______

6 on the ______

7 under the ______

B Complete the sentences.

1 The notebook is ______ the bag.
2 The umbrella is ______ the chair.
3 The chair is ______ the umbrella.
4 The bed is ______ the door and the window.
5 The door is ______ the bed.
6 The lamp is ______ the desk.
7 The dictionary is ______ the watch.

C IN PAIRS Look at your classroom. Say what's on your desk, next to the door and in front of the window.

READING

A IN PAIRS Look at the pictures on page 65 of the Activity Bank. Find three differences between them.

B 2.07 READING SKILL—Identify the topic Quickly read the webpage and choose a title from the box.

A Place for Teachers | The Rooms at the College | Your Favorite Bedroom

NEW COLLEGE

There are two types of rooms for students.

Single (one student)

There's a bed. There's a window between the door and the bed. There's a desk and a chair in front of the window. There's a small lamp on the desk. There's a small closet next to the bed.

Double (two students)

There are two beds in the room. There's a big window between the two beds. There are two desks and two chairs. They are in front of the window. There's a lamp on each desk. There are two closets behind the door.

C **Read the webpage again. Use the words from the box to complete the summary.**

different one same two

There are two types of rooms: single for ________ student and double for ________ students. There is the ________ furniture in each room. The furniture is in a ________ place in each room.

D **IN PAIRS THINKING SKILL—Brainstorm Draw a picture of your bedroom. Show your partner.**

GRAMMAR *There is / There are*

A **Complete the sentences from READING B.**

1 There ________ a bed.
2 There ________ a small closet next to the bed.
3 There ________ two beds in the room.
4 There ________ two closets behind the door.

B **Complete the table with the correct form of *to be*.**

For one thing:	There	**1**	a	desk.
For two or more things:		**2**	two	desks.

For more practice, go to page 72.

C **Complete the sentences with *is*, *'s* or *are*.**

1 There __'s__ a desk. There ________ two notebooks on the desk.
2 There ________ three laptops on the bed.
3 There ________ a small window next to the door.
4 There ________ five students in the class. There ________ one teacher.

D **IN PAIRS In your notebook, make sentences about your classroom using *There is* / *There are*.**

SPEAKING

A **IN PAIRS Student A: look at your picture. Do not show it to Student B. Make notes on the items in the room. Then switch roles. Use the Confident Communicator box to help you.**

Student A: go to page 65 of the Activity Bank.
Student A: say what's in your room.

Student B: go to page 66 of the Activity Bank.
Student B: draw a picture of the room that's described.

There's a bed. The bed is next to the window.

CONFIDENT COMMUNICATOR
KEEP TALKING

To check you understand, use *Right?* after a statement.
The bed is next to the door. Right?
No, the bed is next to the window.

MAKE IT DIGITAL

Search online for rooms at colleges or in hotels. Then write a short description of one room from your search.

Language and Life

Communication – Hotel Room

FUNCTIONAL LANGUAGE book a hotel

A 2.08 **Read and listen to the conversation. Complete the sentences with words from the box. There are two words you do not need.**

friend hotel single double

Sofia calls a __________ . Sofia asks for a __________ room.

Hotel worker: Good morning. Grand Hotel.
Sofia: Good morning. **I want to book a room for Friday night, please.**
Hotel worker: Sure. Let me see if we have a room. **There's a single room and a double room.**
Sofia: What is a double room?
Hotel worker: It's a room with two beds for two people.
Sofia: **OK. A single room, please.**
Hotel worker: No problem. It's a nice room with two big windows. **What's your name and email, please?**
Sofia: Sofia Lopez. My email is sofial95@newmail.com. **How much is it?**
Hotel worker: **It's $100. Please pay at the hotel on Friday.**
Sofia: **Thank you for your help.**
Hotel worker: **You're welcome.** Goodbye.

MAKE IT REAL

In British English: *double room* = a room with a bed for two people
twin room = a room with two beds for two people

B Add the bold sentences from A to the table.

Hotel guest	Hotel worker
I want to book a room for Friday night, please.	*There's a single room and a double room.*
1	**4**
2	**5**
3	**6**

C 2.09 **Listen to two different examples (A and B) from the hotel worker. Is A or B polite? Circle the answer.**

1 A B **2** A B **3** A B

D IN PAIRS **Take turns reading the conversation in A.**

E IN NEW PAIRS **Repeat the conversation with new information. Take turns as the hotel worker and the hotel guest.**

Student A: go to page 65 of the Activity Bank. Student B: go to page 66 of the Activity Bank.

WRITING a text message

A **Read the text messages and choose *True* or *False*. Correct the false sentences.**

1 Dan is in a hotel. True / False ______

2 The room is small. True / False ______

3 There is a restaurant in the hotel. True / False ______

B **Circle six exclamation marks (!) and four question marks (?) in the texts.**

C **Complete the sentences with *?* or *!*.**

1 Use ____ at the end of a question—not at the beginning.

2 Use ____ at the end of a statement—not at the beginning.

3 Use ____ to show you are very happy or not very happy.

D **Complete the sentences with *?* or *!*.**

1 Is the room small

2 The coffee shop is beautiful

3 This hotel is awesome

4 Where is the clothes store

E **Complete the sentences to describe the places. Then write another sentence. Use your own words or the examples from the box.**

closet	clothes store	coffee shop	quiet
noisy	old	small	

1 *The hotel is noisy. It's very old.*

2 The room … ______

3 The restaurant … ______

F **IN PAIRS Exchange answers. Then take turns to ask and answer the questions. Text your questions and answers to each other if possible.**

MAKE IT DIGITAL

Send two text messages to two different classmates in English.

VOCABULARY review

SCORE: / 5

A Choose the word that is different in each group.

1	beautiful	laptops	old	small
2	brush	modern	transit card	wallet
3	door	ID cards	pens	umbrellas
4	bed	between	desk	window
5	behind	in front of	notebook	under

GRAMMAR review

SCORE: / 5

A Complete the sentences.

1 Where __________ you from? I'm from Japan.
2 Who __________ he? He's my teacher.
3 There's a brush and __________ ID card.
4 The chair is next __________ the window.
5 There __________ three windows and two doors.

6–10 correct: You can describe places and where things are, introduce your partner, and talk about your things. You can use *be* information questions, *a*/*an* singular and plural nouns and *There is*/*There are*.
0–5 correct: Look again at the Vocabulary and Grammar sections in the unit.

TOTAL SCORE: / 10

WHAT DO YOU KNOW NOW? Look back at page 15 and add the words you know now to the box.

FOLLOW A PRO ONLINE TEACHER

A Circle useful things for an online teacher.

chair desk dictionary internet laptop phone transit card

B 2.10 Listen and check your answers in A.

C 2.10 Listen again and complete the notes.

Name: *Angela*
Nationality: __________
Language: __________
Job: __________
Nationality of students: __________ and __________
Age of students: __________ to __________ years old

D IN GROUPS Discuss. Are the sentences true for you? Change the sentences to make them true for you.

- I'm an online student.
- There are online teachers in my city.
- An online class is fun.

UNIT 3

Life and Work

WHAT DO YOU ALREADY KNOW?

1 Think about your calendar or planner. Complete the boxes.

2 IN PAIRS Share and compare your details. Add your partner's information to the boxes, if possible.

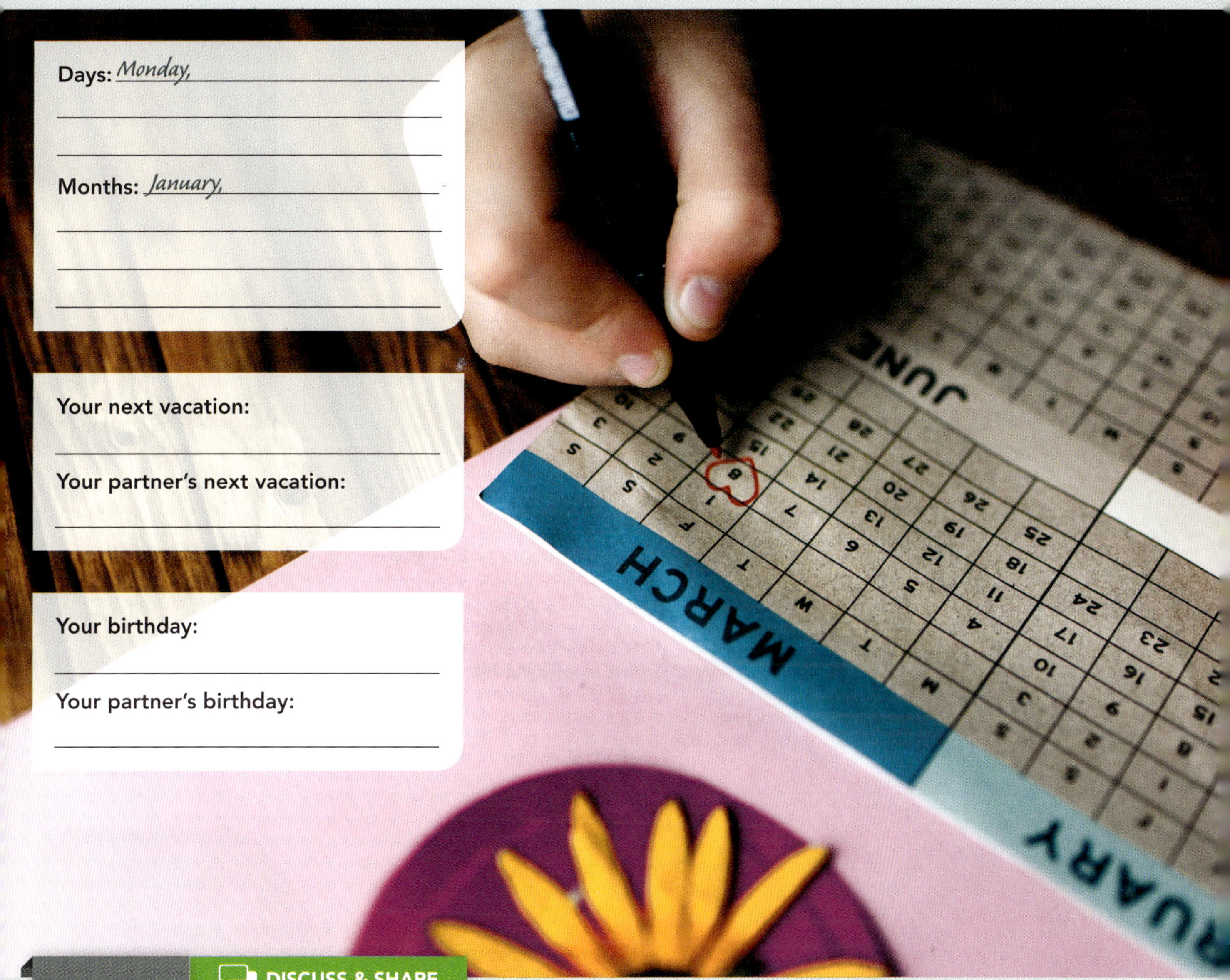

Days: *Monday,* ______________________

____

____

Months: *January,* ______________________

____

____

____

Your next vacation:

____

Your partner's next vacation:

____

Your birthday:

____

Your partner's birthday:

____

VIDEO

DISCUSS & SHARE

3 IN GROUPS Watch the video and answer the question.

SYM Birthdays—party or no party?

In this unit, you will ...

- share information about people in your class, use the simple present, use adverbs of frequency.
- use thinking skills: evaluate and analyze.
- read about the world of work and a hotel.
- use strategies to ask questions to repair a conversation, ask questions to check understanding and agree with an affirmative statement to continue a conversation.
- use communication skills to plan to meet and write an online post.
- learn skills to record vocabulary.

LESSON 1 Jobs

VOCABULARY jobs

A **IN GROUPS** Ask and answer the question *What do you do?*

A: What do you do? *B: I'm a student.*

B **Match the pictures with jobs from the box. Write the words under the pictures.**

chef doctor lawyer manager pilot police officer teacher waiter/waitress

1

______

2

______

3

______

4

______

5

______

6

______

7

______

8

______

C 3.01 **Listen and check your answers to B. Then listen again and repeat.**

MAKE IT YOURS

IN GROUPS Make a list of jobs you know. Use a dictionary to help you.

READING

A **Look at the pictures. Discuss what jobs you think the people do.**

B 3.02 **READING SKILL—Scan for jobs** **Read the texts and check your answers. Then answer the question. What other jobs are in the texts?**

______

The World of Work

Hi, I'm Marie. I **live** in the city. I'm a waitress. I **don't work** in a restaurant. I work in a café. I meet new people every day. It's fun! I'm also a teacher. I **teach** Chinese in a school. The students are nice. I **like** my jobs.

Hello, I'm Gino. I **don't work**. I'm a student. I **go** to college by bus. My brother is a pilot. He **goes** to work by car. He **speaks** three languages: Italian, French and English. He **doesn't speak** Chinese. He **likes** his job. We **live** in an apartment.

C **Read the texts again. Choose the word to complete the sentences.**

1. Marie **speaks** / **doesn't speak** Chinese. She **likes** / **doesn't like** her jobs.
2. Gino **works** / **doesn't work**. He **goes** / **doesn't go** to college.
3. Gino's brother **speaks** / **doesn't speak** Chinese. He **likes** / **doesn't like** his job.
4. Gino and his brother **live** / **don't live** in an apartment.

D **IN GROUPS THINKING SKILL—Evaluate** **Decide which job in the texts you like more. Why?**

GRAMMAR simple present statements

A Complete the table with bold words from READING A.

Subject Pronouns	Verb	
Affirmative		
I	go	to college by bus.
	like	my jobs.
He	speaks	three languages.
	1 ______________	to work by car.
	2 ______________	his job.
Negative		
I	don't work	in a restaurant.
He	**3** ______________ speak	Chinese.

B Look at the table and complete the rules for simple present statements.

1 For affirmative sentences with *He/She/It*:
- add *–s* to regular verbs.
- add ________ to irregular verbs ending with *–o*.

2 For negative sentences with *I/You/We/They*, add *don't* before the verb.
3 For negative sentences with *He/She/It*, add ________ before the verb.

For more practice, go to page 73.

C 3.03 Choose the word to complete the description. Then listen and check.

I **live** / **lives** in Lima. I **don't** / **doesn't** work. I'm a student. I **go** / **goes** to college by bike. I **speak** / **speaks** two languages: English and Spanish. My sister **works** / **doesn't work**. She's a doctor. She **don't** / **doesn't** live in Lima. She **live** / **lives** in New York.

D Write sentences in your notebook using the prompts from the box.

I'm a/an	I live in	I work in	I speak	I don't speak	I go to work/college by

SPEAKING

A IN PAIRS Take turns to say your sentences from GRAMMAR D. Make a note of your partner's answers. Use the Confident Communicator box to help you.

B IN GROUPS Share information about the people in your group/class.

CONFIDENT COMMUNICATOR
REPAIR IT

To repair the conversation, ask questions:
Can you say that again, please? How do you spell engineer?
How do you say that? What does apartment *mean?*

VOCABULARY prepositions of time

A Student A: read the text below. Student B: read the text on page 66 of the Activity Bank.

I go to work by bus **in** the morning. I start work **at** 7:00 a.m. I work in an office. I go to college **on** Wednesday and **on** Thursday. The class is **1** ______ the evening. It starts **2** ______ 6:00 p.m. and ends **3** ______ 8:00 p.m. I study **4** ______ the weekend.

B Take turns to read your text to your partner. (Do not show your partner the text.) Listen to your partner and complete your text.

C Write the correct preposition: *at*, *in* or *on*. Then circle examples from the text.

1

______

2

______

3

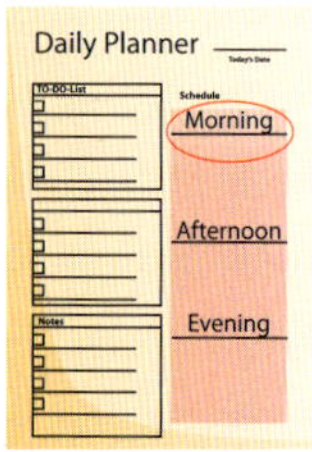

______

LISTENING

A IN PAIRS Look at the picture and discuss the questions: Who are the people? Where are they? What is the conversation about?

B 3.04 Listen and check your ideas from A.

C 3.04 LISTENING SKILL—Listen for names, dates and numbers Listen again and complete Anthony's notes.

Name: Mario

Job: waiter / manager—in the morning / evening

Routine: Mario goes to college in the morning / afternoon and studies in the morning / afternoon. He works in his uncle's shop on Wednesday / the weekend—from 12:00 p.m. to 9:00 p.m.

D 3.05 Listen to the next part. Complete Mario's questions.

1 Does the restaurant open on ______ ?
2 Do the waiters speak ______ ?

E THINKING SKILL—Analyze Do you think Mario gets the job? Why?

MAKE IT REAL

People often say *about* for a time that is not exact.
The waiters finish ***about*** *11. = The waiters finish at 10:50/10:55/11:05/11:10.*
People do not always say *o'clock*, *a.m.* or *p.m.* after the time.
The waiters start work at six.

GRAMMAR *yes/no* questions with simple present

A Match the phrases to make questions and answers from LISTENING B.

1 Do you	open on Sunday?	Yes, they **do**.
2 Does the restaurant	speak English?	No, it **doesn't**.
3 Do the waiters	go to college every day?	No, I **don't**.

B Complete the table with *Do, Does, don't* and *doesn't*. Then add the example questions from A.

Simple Present Questions			
1	you/we/they	+ infinitive …?	e.g., **3**
2	he/she/it	+ infinitive …?	e.g., **4**
Short Answers			
Yes,	I/you/we/they	**5**	
	he/she/it	does.	
No,	I/you/we/they	**6**	
	he/she/it	**7**	

For more practice, go to page 73.

C Find and correct one error in each question. Then complete the short answers.

1 Do your brother study in the afternoon? Yes, he does.
2 Does she goes to college on Wednesday? No, she ____________ .
3 Does you work on Saturday? Yes, I ____________ .
4 Do they starts work at 7:00 p.m.? No, they ____________ .

D IN PAIRS Take turns to ask and answer the questions in C. Use different short answers. Change the subject (*your brother–you; she–they*).

PRONUNCIATION word stress in questions

A 3.06 Listen to the conversations and underline the stressed words.

Conversation 1
Do they <u>speak</u> English?
Yes, they <u>do</u>. / No, they don't.

Conversation 2
Does it open in the mornings?
Yes, it does. / No, it doesn't.

B 3.06 Listen again and repeat.

SPEAKING

A Write five simple present *yes/no* questions in your notebook.

B IN GROUPS Take turns to ask and answer your questions. Use the Confident Communicator box to help you.

CONFIDENT COMMUNICATOR
KEEP TALKING

To continue the conversation and check you understand, ask questions:
Is that right? *Is that OK?*

LESSON 3 Routines

VOCABULARY daily activities

A Write the activities from the box under the correct picture.

drink coffee | eat breakfast | get up at 6 a.m. | go to bed | take a shower

1  ______________

2  ______________

3  ______________

4  ______________

5  ______________

B 3.07 Listen, check and repeat.

C Match the verbs (1–5) to the words (a–e) to make phrases.

1 drink ______ a at 8:00 a.m.
2 eat ______ b a bath
3 get up ______ c tea
4 go to ______ d college
5 take ______ e lunch

D IN PAIRS Write five sentences describing your routine. Then talk about your routine.

I get up at 7:30 a.m. I take a shower.

READING

A 3.08 READING SKILL—Recognize different text types Quickly read the text. What type of text is it?

job advertisement | online article | message

The **24-365** Hotel

11:24

Welcome! I'm Michael Olson and I'm the manager. The hotel is 150 years old. It has 200 rooms, two restaurants and a café. About 400 people work here. It's a big hotel.
We are **always** busy. The hotel is **never** closed. It is open 24 hours a day for 365 days a year. There are **always** guests at the hotel. Guests **usually** stay for one week or two weeks. Families **often** stay here in July and August.

Tourists **often** visit the hotel to eat lunch or dinner. The restaurants are very popular on weekends. There is **rarely** a free table!
Our chefs are excellent. They make excellent food. The waiters and waitresses speak different languages. One waiter speaks five languages! People **sometimes** visit the hotel for work meetings. They drink coffee and talk about work. Visitors love the hotel.

B **Read the text again. Write the numbers from the text next to the descriptions below.**

1 age of the hotel ________
2 rooms and restaurants ________
3 people who work there ________
4 days the hotel is open ________
5 languages one waiter speaks ________

C **THINKING SKILL—Analyze** **Discuss as a class. Look at the phrases in VOCABULARY A. What do you think Michael's routine is? Describe his day.**

I think Michael goes to work at 6 a.m. He has breakfast at the hotel. He ...

GRAMMAR adverbs of frequency

A **Add the bold adverbs from the reading text to the diagram.**

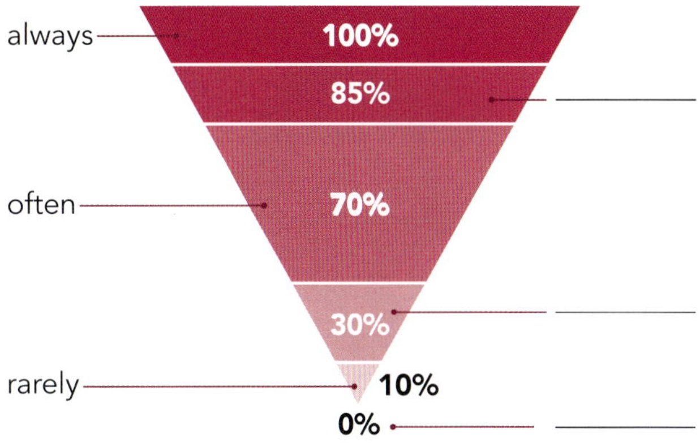

B **Look at the sentences below and underline the two verbs. Then complete the rules.**

1 We are always busy. The hotel never closes.
2 Put the adverb (e.g., *always*):
- before / after the verb *to be*.
- before / after other verbs.

For more practice, go to page 74.

C **Complete the sentences with the correct adverb.**

1 I *often* (70%) go to work by car, but I ________ (30%) go by bus.
2 I don't like baths. I ________ (100%) take a shower.
3 I ________ (0%) eat breakfast. I eat a big lunch.
4 I ________ (85%) study every day, but today I'm at work.
5 I ________ (10%) drink coffee. I prefer tea.

D **IN PAIRS** **Change the sentences in C to be true for you.**

SPEAKING

A **Complete the sentences with the correct adverb and time for your routine.**

- I ________ take a shower________ .
- I ________ get up before ________ .
- I ________ eat breakfast at ________ .
- I ________ drink coffee ________ .
- I ________ go to bed after ________ .

B **IN GROUPS** **Take turns to say your sentences and then discuss the question. Use the Confident Communicator box to help you. Are your routines the same or different?**

CONFIDENT COMMUNICATOR
KEEP TALKING

To continue the conversation, you can agree with an affirmative statement:
I always drink coffee. = *Me, too!* (*I always drink coffee.*)
or agree with a negative statement:
I rarely/never drink coffee. = *Me neither!* (*I rarely/never drink coffee.*)

Language and Life

Communication – Meet Someone

FUNCTIONAL LANGUAGE plan to meet

A 3.09 **Listen to the conversation. Are the speakers friends?**

B 3.09 **Listen again. Circle the correct option to complete Sofia's notes.**

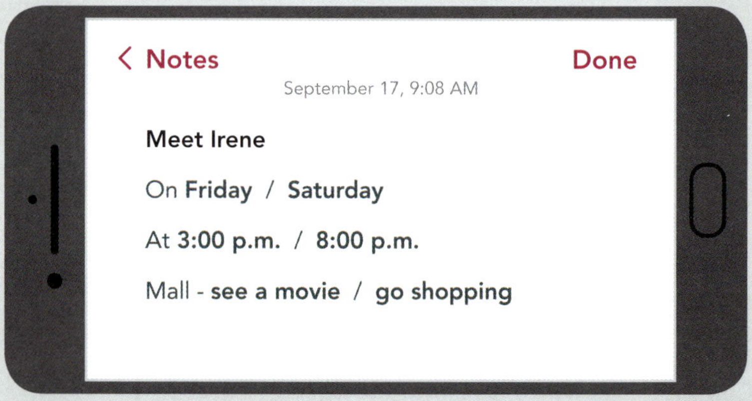

C 3.09 **Listen again. Add three examples of *Let's* and *How about* to the table.**

Let's (= Let us)	+ infinitive.	*Let's go to the mall.* 1 ______ 2 ______
How about	+ time? + day?	*How about Saturday?* 3 ______

D Look at the table again. Then circle to complete the sentences.

1 Use the phrases with friends / people you do not know.
2 *Let's* ... is a sentence / question.
3 *Let's* is a contraction of *Let* + *us* / *is*.
4 *How about* is a sentence / question.
5 Use / Do not use a preposition of time after *How about*.

E 3.10 **Listen and underline the stressed words. Then listen again and repeat.**

Let's go to the mall.

Let's see a movie.

F IN PAIRS Complete the conversation with your own words. Then practice the conversation.

A: Hi. Are you free on Thursday? Let's ______ .

B: Sorry. I work on Thursdays. I study in the evening. How about ______ ? I'm free in the morning.

A: Me, too. How about ______ ?

B: OK. Let's ______ .

A: No. Let's ______ .

WRITING a post

A Read the posts and answer the questions. Who is a teacher? Who are students?

English **101**

Welcome to your English class! I'm Roger. I'm your teacher. Nice to meet you! There are 95 students in this online language course. Let's say hello!

Hi, Roger! Hi, everyone! I'm Mia. I'm from Salvador. I'm a student. I always go to classes in the mornings. **I usually go by bus, but sometimes I walk.** Do you live in my city? Let's start a study group! **I'm free in the evenings but not in the afternoons.**

Hello Mia! My name's Paola and I'm a police officer. How about Monday? I'm free at 7:00 p.m. Let's meet at the coffee shop across from the train station. **It's quiet and the coffee is great.**
1 day ago

B Look at the bold sentences. Which word ...

1. joins two affirmative phrases or clauses? __________
2. joins an affirmative and a negative phrase or clause? __________
3. comes after a comma? __________

C Complete the sentences with *and* or *but*.

1. I'm a student __________ I'm a manager.
2. I rarely work in the evening, __________ sometimes I work on the weekend.
3. I like my city, __________ I don't like my apartment.
4. I go to bed at 11:00 p.m. __________ I get up at 7:00 a.m.

D Prepare a reply for Roger's post.

1. Write sentences with:
   - your name __________
   - where you live __________
   - where and when you work/study __________
2. Join two sentences with *and*. Join two sentences with *but*. __________
3. Arrange to meet your classmates. __________

E IN PAIRS Exchange your sentences. Check that your partner includes all the points in D.

F Read your sentences again and make any changes. Then write your reply in a paragraph.

MAKE IT DIGITAL

Go online and search for online courses. What courses are there? Is there a course you like?

VOCABULARY review

SCORE: / 5

A Match the sentence beginnings (1–5) to the sentence ends (a–e).

1 A chef works ______
2 A pilot flies ______
3 I don't eat ______
4 I usually go ______
5 I always get ______

a up at 6:00 a.m.
b to bed early.
c in a restaurant.
d a plane to different places.
e breakfast on the weekend.

GRAMMAR review

SCORE: / 5

A Find and correct the error in each sentence.

1 The store closes on 7:00 p.m. ______
2 They goes to school by bus. ______
3 Does they start work at 9:00 a.m.? Yes, they do. ______
4 I eat lunch never. ______
5 Do you always eat breakfast? No, I does. ______

6–10 correct: You can talk about jobs, describe your partner, talk about time and daily activities, and describe your daily routine. You can use simple present statements, *yes/no* questions with simple present and adverbs of frequency.
0–5 correct: Look again at the Vocabulary and Grammar sections in the unit.

TOTAL SCORE: / 10

WHAT DO YOU KNOW NOW? Look back at the unit and review the language you know now.

STUDY SKILLS RECORDING VOCABULARY

A IN GROUPS Think of three ways to make vocabulary notes. Tell your group.

B Look at the ways below. Are these ways you use?

1

2
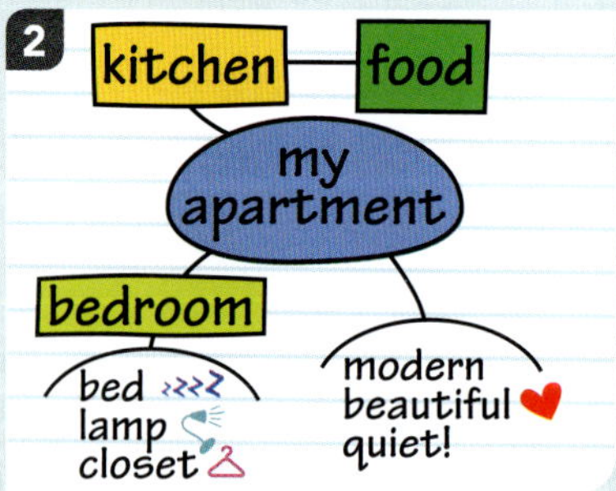

3
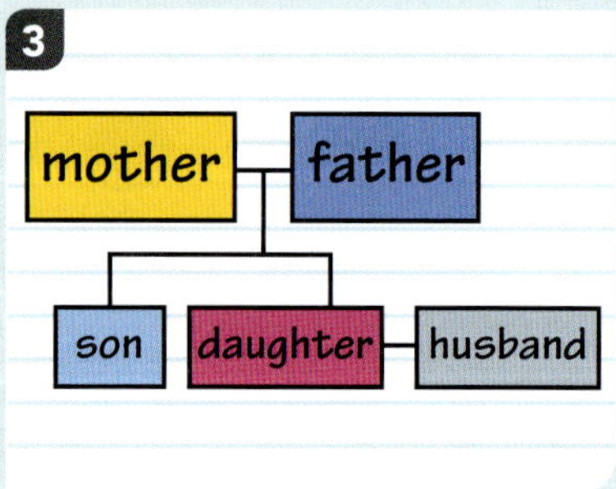

C Choose one way (or more) from B and make notes on vocabulary from Unit 1, 2 or 3.

D IN GROUPS Show your vocabulary notes to the group. Then say the words. Don't look at your notes.

UNIT 4 My City

WHAT DO YOU ALREADY KNOW?

1 Think about things you can buy in stores or malls. Write words that you know in the box.

2 IN PAIRS Share and compare your information. Add more words to the box, if possible.

Clothes: *dress,* ______________

____

____

Technology: *laptop,* ______________

____

____

Accessories: *bags,* ______________

____

____

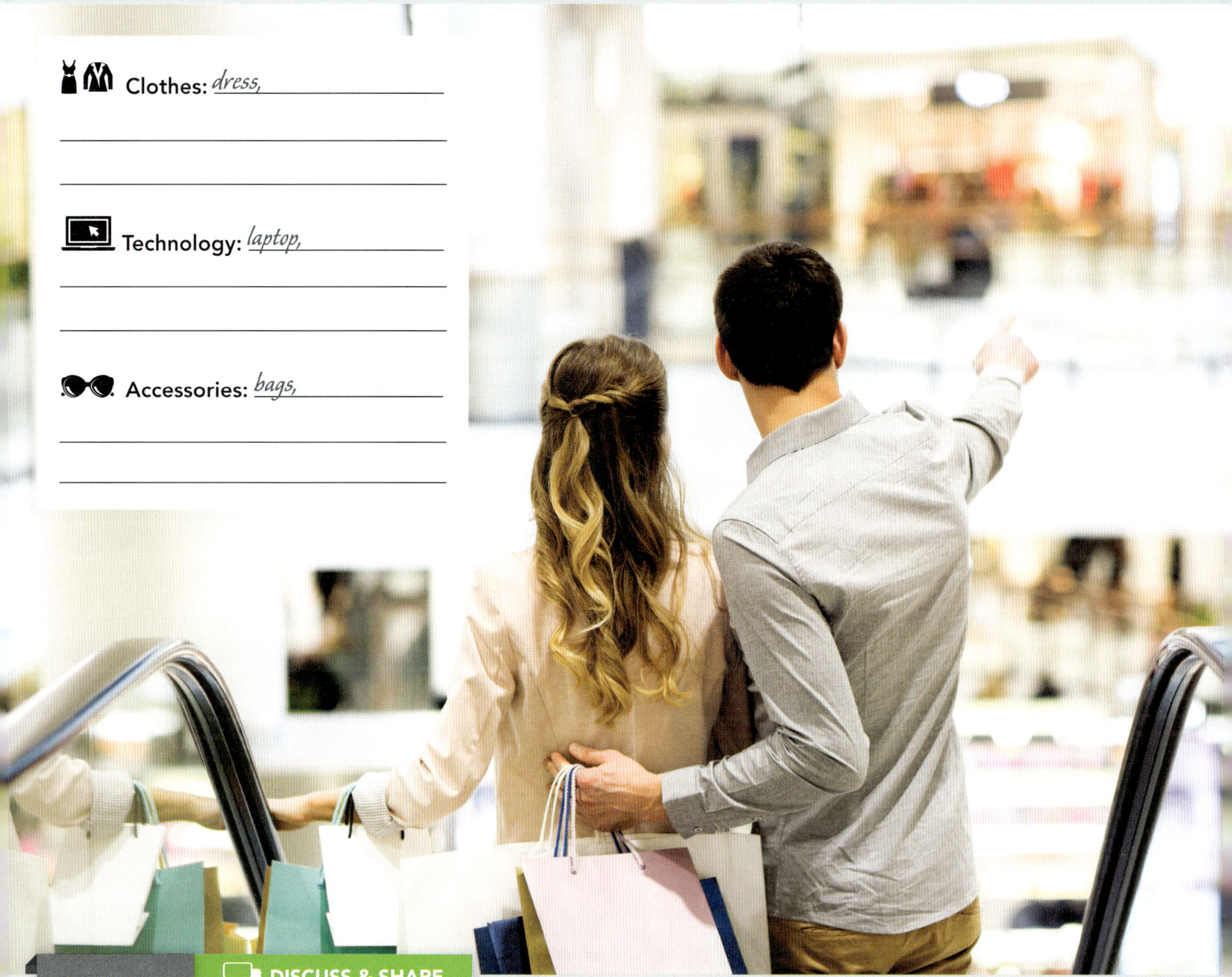

VIDEO

DISCUSS & SHARE

3 IN GROUPS Watch the video and answer the question.

SYM Online shopping or store shopping?

In this unit, you will ...

- ask and answer questions about a tour, ask for and give directions and talk about your clothes.
- use thinking skills: analyze and evaluate.
- read about a city tour.
- use strategies to practice taking turns, finish a conversation in a natural way and reply when you don't know the answer.
- use communication skills to practice buying things and write a description of a store.
- follow a tour guide to learn about their job and the skills needed to be in this industry.

LESSON 1 Places

VOCABULARY places in a city

A IN PAIRS Write the correct phrase from the box under the pictures.

buy a book	buy a drink	eat dinner	get a bus	get a degree
get help	get money	go for a walk	learn about the past	stay on vacation

1 bus station

____

2 park

____

3 ATM

____

4 hotel

____

5 museum

____

6 hospital

____

7 university

____

8 bookstore

____

9 coffee shop

____

10 restaurant

____

B 4.01 Listen, check your answers to A and repeat.

C IN PAIRS Think about your hometown and tell your partner about the places in A.

There's a coffee shop and a park.

MAKE IT YOURS

What other places do you often go to in your hometown? Use your dictionary to find new words.

READING

A 4.02 Quickly read the text in B. Choose a description.

information about a city tour   review of a restaurant   advertisement for a museum

B Read the text again. What places from VOCABULARY A are in the text?

What places does the tour visit?
The tour goes to the important places in the city. For example, there are two museums in the city. There's the history museum and the science museum. The museums are free on Tuesdays. Tourists always love the history museum.

Where does the tour start and finish?
Everywhere! Tourists get on the bus at the bus station or at a bus stop in the city. People get off the bus and go to a museum or have lunch in a restaurant. Then people get on the bus again later. It's very easy!

When does the first tour start?
The first tour leaves the bus station at 7:00 a.m. The last tour is at 9:00 p.m. There is a new tour every hour.

Where do I buy tickets?
We sell tickets at the bus station, online and on the bus. Hotels also sell tickets.

How much do the tickets cost?
The tickets cost $20 for adults and $10 for children or students.

C **READING SKILL—Locate information in a text** Read the text again. Choose *True* or *False*. Correct the false sentences.

1 The museums are free on one day. True / False
2 People have lunch on the bus. True / False
3 The last tour is at 7:00 p.m. True / False
4 People buy tickets online. True / False

D **THINKING SKILL—Analyze** Do you like bus tours? Explain why or why not.

GRAMMAR simple present information questions

A Complete the questions from the text.

1 ________ does the tour start and finish?
2 ________ does the tour visit?
3 ________ does the first tour start?
4 ________ much do the tickets cost?

B Match the question words (1–4) to the information (a–d).

1 how much	**a** place
2 what	**b** time
3 when	**c** general information
4 where	**d** price

C Complete the table with *do* or *does*.

Question Word	*do/does*	Subject	Verb
Where	**1**	the tour	start and finish?
What	**2**	the tour	visit?
When	**3**	the first tour	start?
Where	**4**	I	buy tickets?
How much	**5**	the tickets	cost?

For more practice, go to page 74.

D Complete the questions.

1 *Where* do you go on the weekend?
2 What ________ tourists visit in your town?
3 ________ does your favorite coffee shop open?
4 How much ________ a bus ticket cost in your town?

E **IN PAIRS** Answer the questions in D. Discuss.

SPEAKING

A **IN PAIRS** Read the information about a tour. Take turns to ask and answer questions from GRAMMAR A.

Student A: look at the information on page 65 of the Activity Bank.
Student B: look at the information on page 67 of the Activity Bank.

B **IN GROUPS** Compare and discuss the two tours in the Activity Bank and the tour in READING A. Choose your favorite. Use the Confident Communicator box to help you.

CONFIDENT COMMUNICATOR
KEEP TALKING

To take turns with your partner, ask and answer:
Is it my turn?
Yes, it's your turn.
No, it's my turn.

LESSON 2 Directions

LISTENING

A 4.03 **Listen and match the conversations (1–3) to the places (a–c).**

1	Conversation 1	**a**	hotel
2	Conversation 2	**b**	museum
3	Conversation 3	**c**	train station

B 4.03 LISTENING SKILL—Understand key words **Listen again and number the directions in the correct order.**

Conversation 1

_____ it's on the left
_____ go straight
_____ take the second right
_____ turn left

Conversation 2

_____ take the #5 bus—about 10 minutes
_____ bus station
_____ go straight

Conversation 3

_____ bookstore on left
_____ between coffee shop and bookstore
_____ take the first left
_____ turn right

C IN GROUPS THINKING SKILL—Evaluate **Discuss and compare the ways you remember directions or information. Do you repeat information? Do you write notes or take pictures?**

MAKE IT REAL

Use *Excuse me* before you ask questions to people you don't know.
Excuse me, *is the park near here?*

VOCABULARY prepositions of place 2

A **Write a phrase from the box under each picture.**

across from	between	next to	on	on the corner of	on the left/right

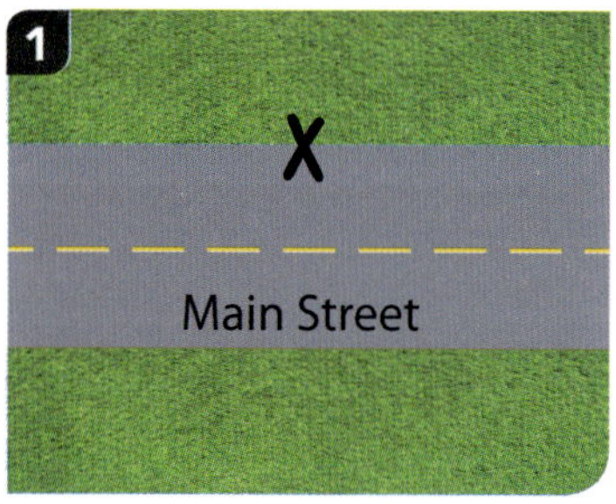

____

____

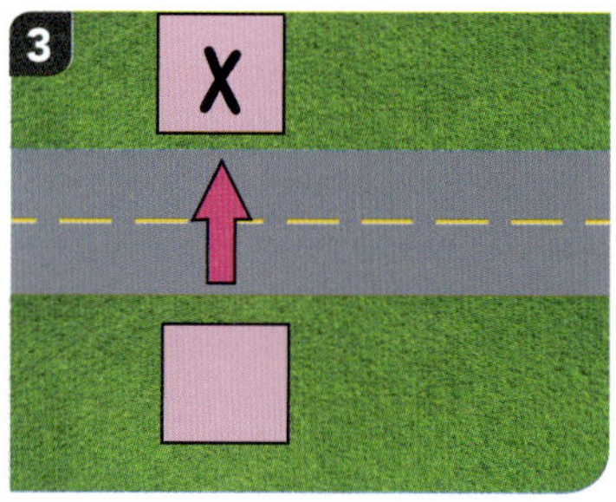

____

____

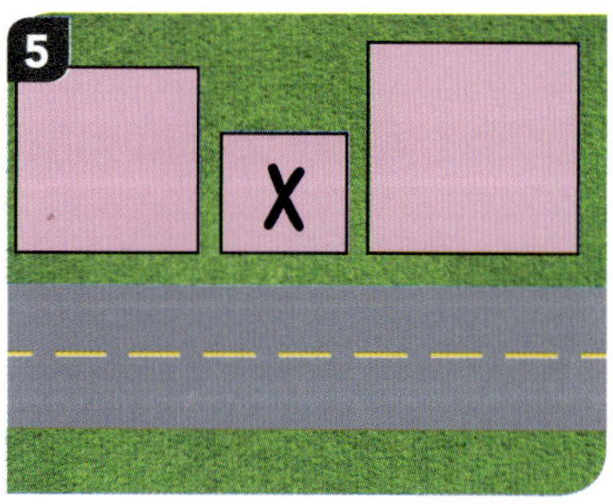

____

____

B 4.04 **Listen and check your answers to A. Then listen and repeat.**

C IN PAIRS **Complete the activity. Then switch roles.**

Student A: close your book.
Student B: say a preposition of place.
Student A: draw a picture that represents the preposition.

GRAMMAR imperatives

A Add the sentences to the table.

Is the train station near here?
It's across from the park.
It's between the park and the school.
Take the second right.
Turn left.

Ask for Directions	Give Directions	Finish Directions
Where's the museum?	*Go straight up this road.*	*The science museum is on the left.*
1	2	4
	3	5

B Underline the verbs in the table in A.

C Choose the correct words to complete the rules.

To give directions:
1 **Start** / **Do not start** the sentence with a verb.
2 **Use** / **Do not use** a subject in the sentence.
To finish directions:
3 **Use** / **Do not use** a subject in the sentence.

For more practice, go to page 75.

D 4.05 Put the words in the correct order. Listen and check your answers.

1 where / the hospital? / me, / Excuse / is *Excuse me, where is the hospital?*
2 this / straight / Go / road. / up ______
3 to / bookstore / The / is / the hotel. / next ______
4 It's / the / corner of / 1st / and Main. / on ______
5 take / Turn left / first / right. / the / and ______

E IN PAIRS Write directions for the questions in D. Use your own ideas or give real directions.

SPEAKING

A IN PAIRS Complete the activity. Choose other places and ask for directions. Use the Confident Communicator box to help you.

Student A and Student B: look at the map on page 66 of the Activity Bank.

Student A: ask for directions to the library. **Student B:** ask for directions to the train station.

CONFIDENT COMMUNICATOR
KEEP TALKING

To finish a conversation in a natural way, it is polite to say *Thanks* or *Thank you* and to reply *No problem* or *You're welcome.*

LESSON 3 Clothes

VOCABULARY clothes

A Write one word from each pair in the box under the pictures (1–5).

dress/skirt   jacket/suit   pants/jeans   shirt/T-shirt   shoes/boots

1 
____

2 
____

3 
____

4 
____

5 
____

B 4.06 Go to page 67 of the Activity Bank.

C **IN GROUPS** Make a list of your clothes in your notebook. Add more information, e.g., style or color.

dressy jacket, new jeans, pink T-shirt

PRONUNCIATION vowel sounds 1

A 4.07 Listen to the vowel sound and the words. Then listen again and repeat.

æ	ɜ	ɝ	iː	uː
jacket	dress	skirt	jeans	shoes

B 4.08 Listen and match the words (1–4) to the correct vowel sound (a–d).

1 boots   **2** pants   **3** shirt   **4** T-shirt

a æ   **b** ɝ   **c** iː   **d** uː

LISTENING

A Look at the pictures. Which people are in a store?

a 

b 

MAKE IT REAL

Stores use numbers, letters or words for sizes.
Numbers: *4, 6, 8, 10, 12, 14, 16, 18, 20*
Letter and words: *XS* (extra small), *S* (small), *M* (medium), *L* (large), *XL* (extra large)

B 4.09 Listen and check. Match the conversations to the pictures in A.

Conversation 1: ________   Conversation 2: ________

C 4.09 **LISTENING SKILL—Identify information** Listen again and complete each sentence.

Conversation 1
1 The clothes are under **$30** / **$20**.
2 The dress **is** / **isn't** the correct size.
3 They **like** / **don't like** the shoes.

Conversation 2
4 The red T-shirt is **$55** / **$15**.
5 The blue T-shirt **is** / **isn't** the correct size.
6 The sister **likes** / **doesn't like** the bags.

D **THINKING SKILL—Evaluate** Do you buy clothes in a store or online? Why?

GRAMMAR *this/that/these/those*

A Complete the sentences from LISTENING B (1–4) with the correct word from the box.

that these this those ×2

1 Do you like _______ blue T-shirt?
2 Look at _______ T-shirts!
3 Look at _______ jacket over there!
4 It's between _______ shoes and _______ bags.

B Read the sentences in A and complete the rules.

1 Use _______ and _______ for singular nouns, e.g., *T-shirt.*
2 Use _______ and _______ for plural nouns, e.g., *T-shirts.*

C Go to page 69 of the Activity Bank.

D Match the sentence halves.

1 Use *this* and *these* for objects	a not very near to you.
2 Use *that* and *those* for objects	b very near to you.

For more practice, go to page 76.

E Complete the sentences with *this*, *that*, *these* or *those*.

1 ___*This*___ is my favorite shirt and _______ are my favorite jeans.
2 Look at _______ dress in the window over there! It's beautiful. _______ shoes are pretty, too.
3 I like _______ jeans over there. They're next to _______ yellow bag.
4 _______ skirts over here are expensive. _______ skirts by the door are cheap.

F IN PAIRS Write sentences describing:

1 your clothes using *this* or *these*.
2 your partner's clothes using *that* or *those*.

This shirt is new. These shoes are size 8. That long skirt is nice. Those jeans are loose.

SPEAKING

A IN PAIRS Role-play. Then switch roles and repeat. Use the Confident Communicator box to help you.

Student A: close your book.
Student B: point to clothes on the page (or your clothes) and ask *What's this/these?*
Student A: answer with *That's … / Those are …*

CONFIDENT COMMUNICATOR
REPAIR IT

To help you reply when you don't know the answer, say:
✓ *I think so.*
? *I'm not sure. / I don't know.*
✗ *I don't think so.*

Language and Life

Communication – Shop

FUNCTIONAL LANGUAGE buy things

A Look at the pictures and quickly read the conversation. What things (1–6) do the people not talk about?

1

2

3

4

5

6

Ally: Excuse me. How much is this laptop?
Bob: It's $ ________ . It isn't new. It's old and slow.
Ally: Oh, OK. No, thank you.
Cate: **How much** are these black boots?
Bob: They're $ ________ .
Cate: **Oh, that's expensive.**
Bob: Do you like these brown boots? These are only $15.
Cate: Oh, yes. Could I take those, please?
Bob: Sure. That's $ ________ , please.
Cate: Here you go.
Bob: Thanks.
Ally: How much are the books in this box?
Bob: They're $ ________ each.
Ally: **Could I take these two books, please?**
Bob: **No problem.** That's $ ________ , please.
Ally: Here you go.
Bob: Thank you. Have a great day!

B 4.10 **Read and listen to the conversation. Complete the prices in A.**

C Look at the diagram. Add more bold examples from the conversation in your notebook.

FIRST QUESTION AND ANSWER	**Buyer** Excuse me. How much is this laptop? →	**Seller** It's $50.
↓ **DECISION**	**Yes** Could I take those, please?	**No** No, thank you.
↓ **PAYING**	**Seller** Sure. That's $15, please. →	**Buyer** Here you go.

D Put the conversation in the correct order.

_____ Oh, that's expensive. How much are these **small notebooks**?
_____ Here you go.
_____ It's $**10**.
_____ Sure. That's $**6**, please.
__1__ Excuse me, how much is this **big notebook**?
_____ OK. Could I take **two small notebooks**, please?
_____ They're $3 each.

E 4.11 Listen and check. Then listen again and repeat.

F IN PAIRS Take turns to be the seller and the buyer. Choose something to buy from the box. Repeat the conversation in C with the new object and price.

jeans $40 | laptop $200 | notebook $4 | pens $2 | shoes $25 | skirt $20

WRITING a description

A Read the description and answer the questions in your notebook.

Ellie — 12. June 2019

My favorite store is Alfred's. It's a **small** store on Park Street. It's next to a **modern** hotel. The store sells **old** clothes, computers, jewelry and books. It's an **interesting** store. The things are usually **cheap**.

1 What is the store's name?
2 Where is the store?
3 What does the store sell?
4 How much are things in the store?

B Choose the correct word to complete the sentence.

A noun / verb follows the bold adjectives in **A**.

C Add the adjectives to the sentences in your notebook.

1 This is an website. (*interesting*)
2 Those are the books. (*cheap*)
3 It's a store. (*busy*)
4 My sister buys shoes. (*expensive*)

D Prepare a description of your favorite store. Write answers to the questions in A. Include adjectives.

E IN PAIRS Exchange your descriptions in D. Check that your partner answers the questions in A and uses adjectives correctly.

F Write your description in a paragraph.

MAKE IT DIGITAL

Search online for descriptions of stores in your city. Do you agree with the descriptions (of stores you know)? Are there new stores in your city?

VOCABULARY review

SCORE: / 5

A Choose the correct words.

1 Let's get something to drink at the **coffee shop** / **bus station**.
2 The store is on the **between** / **corner of** Main Street and First Avenue.
3 Wow! These clothes aren't expensive. They're **cheap** / **tight**.
4 The bookstore is **on the left** / **between** the restaurant and the bus station.
5 I like these **dress** / **boots**.

GRAMMAR review

SCORE: / 5

A Choose the words to complete the sentences.

1 **These** / **This** are my new shoes. Do you like them?
2 Where **do** / **does** you buy your clothes?
3 **What** / **Where** is the restaurant?
4 **Take** / **Go** straight up this road.
5 The museum is **across from** / **between the** park.

6–10 correct: You can talk about places in a city, give directions, describe where places are, and talk about clothes. You can use simple present information questions, imperatives and *this/that/these/those*.
0–5 correct: Look again at the Vocabulary and Grammar sections in the unit.

TOTAL SCORE: / 10

WHAT DO YOU KNOW NOW? Look back at page 35 and add the words you know now to the box.

FOLLOW A PRO TOUR GUIDE

A Complete the diagram about a tour guide. Use the verbs in the box.

answers gives speaks

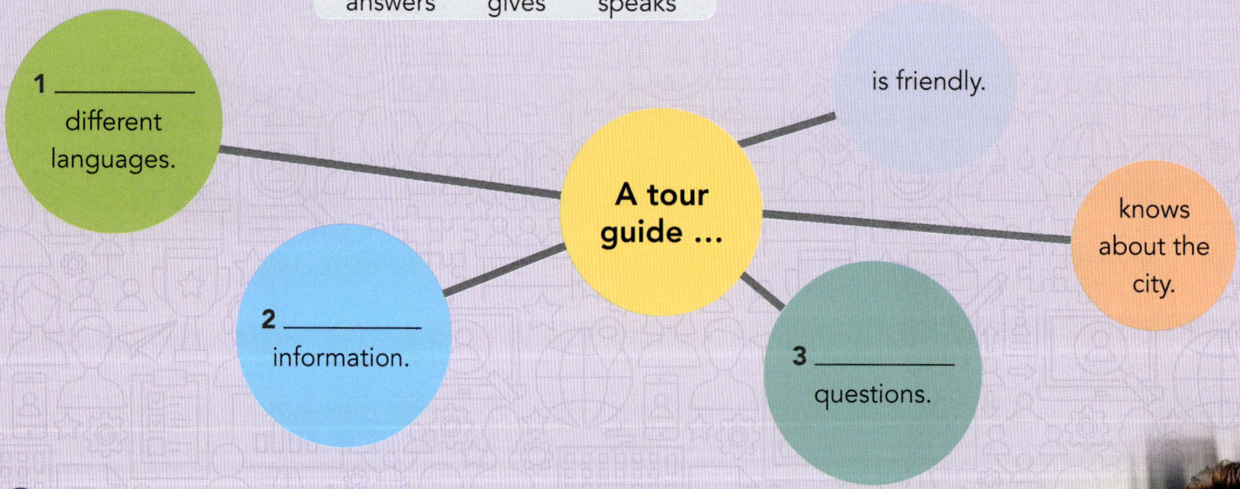

B 4.12 Listen and number the points in the order you hear them.

_______ knows about the city
_______ is friendly
_______ answers questions
_______ speaks different languages
_______ gives information

C Discuss the questions as a class.

1 Does your city have tour guides? Where do they work?
2 Is it important to have a friendly tour guide?
3 Do tour guides get a lot of money?

UNIT 5 Free Time

WHAT DO YOU ALREADY KNOW?

1 Think about the activities people enjoy in different types of weather. Write words that you know in the boxes.

2 IN PAIRS Share and compare your information. Add more words to the boxes, if possible.

Activities in hot weather: *surfing,* ____________

____

____

____

Activities in cool weather: *skiing,* ____________

____

____

____

VIDEO

DISCUSS & SHARE

3 IN GROUPS Watch the video and answer the question.

SYM Hot weather or cool weather?

In this unit, you will ...

- talk about what you can/can't do, talk about different people's objects and discuss activities people are doing.
- use thinking skills: analyze, recall and brainstorm.
- read an online advertisement for college courses.
- use strategies to add explanations or extra information to continue a conversation, respond to others when playing a game and use expressions to show you understand.
- use communication skills to make recommendations and write a blog post.
- learn skills to practice vocabulary.

VOCABULARY free-time activities

A 5.01 **Listen and look at the pictures. Write the numbers of the activities you do not hear.**

2,

1

2

3

4

5

6

7

8

B Write the activities from the box under the pictures in A.

bake a cake	dance salsa	do karate	draw pictures
drive a car	play an instrument	ride a horse	swim 1,500 m

C 5.02 **Listen, check and repeat.**

MAKE IT YOURS

Write other activities that you or your friends do in your notebook. Use your dictionary to help you.

LISTENING

A 5.03 **LISTENING SKILL—Listen for main idea Listen and choose the correct descriptions.**

1 The conversation is on a radio show / in a classroom.
2 The people are new students at a college / friends at a sports event.

B 5.03 **Listen again. What activities from VOCABULARY A do you hear?**

draw,

C 5.03 **Listen again and complete the table.**

Name	Can ✓	Can't ✗
Francesca		
Javier		

D THINKING SKILL—Analyze Categorize the activities from VOCABULARY A so they are true for you.

Cheap	Expensive	Easy	Hard

GRAMMAR *can/can't*

A 5.04 **Complete the sentences from LISTENING A with *can* or *can't*. Listen and check.**

1 __________ you draw? Yes, I __________.
2 __________ you swim? No, I __________. I __________ swim, I __________ do karate.
3 __________ you ride a horse? No, I __________. I __________ drive a car.

B Look at the questions and answers in A. Match to complete the rules.

1 To make *Can* questions, use
2 To give short answers, use
3 To make *can* statements, use

a *yes/no* + pronoun + *can/can't*.
b pronoun + *can/can't* + infinitive.
c *can* + pronoun + infinitive.

For more practice, go to page 76.

C Complete the sentences.

1 A: *Can you* do karate? B: __________, I can't.
2 A: __________ you play the piano? B: Yes, I __________.
3 A: Can he swim? B: No, he __________.
4 A: Can they bake a cake? B: __________, they can.
5 I can dance salsa, but I __________ play an instrument.
6 I can ride a horse and I __________ drive a car.

D IN PAIRS Ask and answer the questions in A. Answer the questions for you.

PRONUNCIATION stress in *can/can't*

A 5.05 **Listen and underline the stressed words.**

1 Can you bake a cake? 2 Yes, I can bake a cake. 3 No, I can't bake a cake.

B 5.05 **Listen again and repeat.**

SPEAKING

A Look at the pictures in VOCABULARY A. Put a check (✓) next to the activities you can do and an X (×) next to the activities you can't do.

B IN GROUPS Take turns to ask and answer what you can/can't do. Use the Confident Communicator box to help you.

Find out:
- How many people can do each activity?
- How many people can't do each activity?
- Who can do an activity very well?

I can swim. I swim in a club. I swim in sports competitions.

CONFIDENT COMMUNICATOR
KEEP TALKING

To continue the conversation, add an explanation or extra information:
Can you ride a horse? No, I can't. ***I don't like big animals.***
Can you play the piano? Yes, I can. ***I'm very good.***

VOCABULARY subjects

A **IN PAIRS** **Answer the questions. Do you take other language classes or study other subjects? What are they?**

B **Match the pictures to the classes. Write the class under the picture.**

art | Chinese | creative writing | dance | math | music | science

1 
____

2 
____

3 
____

4 
____

5 
____

6 
____

7 
____

C 5.06 **Listen and check your answers to B. Then listen again and repeat.**

D **IN PAIRS** Student A: **go to page 67 of the Activity Bank. Read the names of the classroom items.** Student B: **try to match each item to a subject.**

E **IN PAIRS** **Discuss. What classes in A do students usually study in high school in your country?**

READING

A **Quickly read the webpage. What type of text is it?**

an advertisement for courses | a letter to students | a story about a family

Students | Classes

Want to study a subject or learn a new hobby? Green Park has the course for you.

Click here to meet our students.

Can you guess what they study?

This is Brad.

This is Brad's dictionary and these are Brad's shoes.

Brad's mother, Linda, is also a student.

This is Linda's notebook and these are Linda's paint brushes.

B 5.07 **READING SKILL—Scan for key words** **Read the Classes webpage on page 49. Add the classes from the box to the text.**

art | Chinese | dance | math | science | writing

Students | Classes

______

What do you know about science? This class is an introduction to biology, chemistry and physics. Our teachers use videos and real-life examples in the classes.

______

Are numbers hard for you? Our excellent teachers explain how to understand numbers. This is a popular class for young and old people.

______

Nǐ hǎo! Join this class and say hello in a new language! Learn how to write and speak Chinese with our friendly Chinese teachers.

______

Can you draw? Everyone can learn to draw! The lessons are at the college, but students often visit places in the city.

______

Tango? Salsa? This course is for beginners. Learn about different dances and practice with our teachers.

______

Do you want to write a story? Students practice different ways of writing and share their stories with the class.

C IN PAIRS THINKING SKILL—Recall List the classes Brad and Linda go to in your notebook.

D Read the text again. Find words that mean:

1 an activity you enjoy (not a job) ______

2 something that lots of people like ______

3 smiles at people and helps people ______

4 people who start something new ______

GRAMMAR possessive 's

A Circle the five bold possessive 's in the text about Brad and his mother.

B Read the sentence and choose the correct meaning:
This is Brad's dictionary and these are Brad's shoes.

Brad: This is my dictionary and these are my shoes. / This isn't my dictionary and these aren't my shoes.

C Choose the word to complete the rule.

1 Add 's **before** / **after** a name or noun.

For more practice, go to page 77.

D Correct the sentences.

1 Are these Brads books? *Are these Brad's books?*

2 Is this Linda notebook? ______

3 This is the teacher dictionary. ______

4 These are my pen's. ______

SPEAKING

A Work in groups of three. Go to page 69 of the Activity Bank and follow the instructions. Use the Confident Communicator box to help you.

B Switch roles and repeat.

CONFIDENT COMMUNICATOR
KEEP TALKING

To continue the game after your partner gives his or her answer, say: *Yes, that's the correct answer! Good job!*
No, sorry. That's not the right answer. Try again.

Weather

VOCABULARY types of weather

A IN PAIRS **Order the weather from 1 (your favorite) to 5 (not your favorite).**

It's **sunny**. _____ It's **windy**. _____ It's **snowy**. _____ It's **rainy**. _____ It's **cloudy**. _____

B 5.08 **Listen and underline the stressed syllable in the bold words in A. Listen again and repeat.**

C **Add the words from the box to the thermometer.**

cool freezing hot

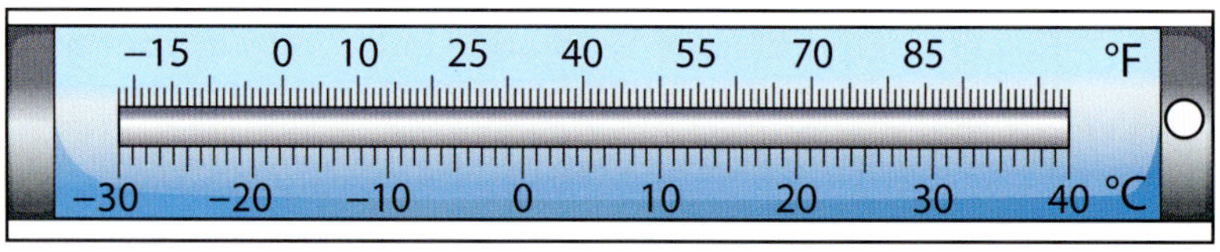

_____________ _____________ _____________

D 5.09 **Listen and check. Listen again and repeat.**

LISTENING

A IN GROUPS **Answer the question. How do you talk to friends in different places? Circle all the ways you use.**

email
letter
phone call
social media
text message
video call

B **Look at the picture. Which way from A are the friends using to communicate?**

C 5.10 **Listen to the conversation and choose the correct option.**

The friends live in **the same** / **different** places and they are doing **the same** / **different** activities.

D 5.10 LISTENING SKILL—Listen for reasons **Listen again and match the sentence beginnings (1–3) to the sentence endings (a–c).**

1 Charlie and his family are at the beach
2 Barney is watching a movie and eating dinner
3 Barney is watching a movie and eating dinner

a because it's very sunny.
b because it's warm.
c because the weather's bad.

E THINKING SKILL—Brainstorm **What other activities can you do in warm or cold weather?**

MAKE IT REAL

Use questions with *like* to ask for a short description.
What's the weather like? It's sunny.
What's the restaurant like? It's nice.

GRAMMAR present progressive statements

A Read the summary of the conversation and underline seven examples of the present progressive. Then answer the questions (1–3).

Andy is swimming in the ocean. Charlie's mom isn't reading a book. She's sleeping. Charlie's dad is practicing Spanish. Barney is watching a movie and eating dinner. Jessica is shopping. Jessica and her friend are getting food for a barbecue. Charlie is having fun.

1 Are the activities in the past? ____________

2 Are the activities in the present? ____________

3 Are the activities happening now? ____________

B Add the verbs from the box to the table.

eat practice shop sleep

		+ *–ing*		
Pronoun	***To be* (+/–)**	**Regular Spelling**	**Irregular Spelling**	
I	'm 'm not	reading. watching TV.	getting coffee. swimming.	having fun. **4** ____________
He/She/It	's isn't	**1** ____________ **2** ____________	**3** ____________	
You/ We/They	are aren't			

C Write the verbs from the table next to the spelling rule.

1 end of verb is consonant, vowel, consonant: double the final consonant and add *–ing* ____________________

2 a final *–e*: delete the final *e* and add *–ing* ____________________

For more practice, go to page 77.

D 5.11 Complete the conversations. Then listen and check.

Conversation 1

A: ___Are___ you ___studying___? (study) B: Yes. We ____________ English. (practice)

Conversation 2

A: ____________ you ____________ lunch? (eat)

B: No, I ____________ lunch. I ____________ coffee with my sister. (eat, have)

E IN PAIRS Take turns to practice the conversations in D. Then write different answers to the questions.

SPEAKING

A IN GROUPS Role-play. What activities are you doing? What are you not doing?

Student A: go to page 69 of the Activity Bank. **Student B:** go to page 65 of the Activity Bank.
Student C: go to page 67 of the Activity Bank. **Student D:** go to page 68 of the Activity Bank.

B Ask and answer questions. Use the Confident Communicator box to help you.

CONFIDENT COMMUNICATOR

KEEP TALKING

To continue the conversation, use an expression to show you understand:

It's beautiful here. Look at the beach. *Wow!*
It's rainy. It's windy. It's very cold. *Oh, no!*

Language and Life

Communication – Your City

FUNCTIONAL LANGUAGE make recommendations

A IN PAIRS Discuss. What do tourists usually do in your city?

B 5.12 Read the blog and guess the missing words. Then listen and check.

One Day in My City

530 Followers

Morning

Visit the ____________ and learn about the city's history. **Go** early because it's free before 10 a.m. **Don't go** on Monday because it's closed!

Afternoon

Go to the ____________. **Swim** in the ocean or **take** a boat trip. **Get** a ____________ at the beach café or at the hotel's coffee shop.

Evening

Eat dinner at Gino's pizzeria. **Reserve** a table because it's always ____________. Then **go** to the park and **watch** a ____________ at the outdoor movie theater.

follow

C 5.13 Listen and discuss. Why are the bold verbs stressed?

1 **Visit** the museum.
2 **Don't go** on Monday.
3 **Go** to the beach.
4 **Swim** in the ocean.
5 **Get** a coffee.
6 **Eat** dinner at Gino's.
7 **Reserve** a table.

D 5.13 Listen again and repeat.

E Think about recommendations for your city. Use the verbs to help you.

Don't …	Go to …	Visit …
Eat …	Look at …	Walk …

F IN PAIRS Share your recommendations about your city.

WRITING a blog

A **Complete the sentences from the blog in FUNCTIONAL LANGUAGE B. Then find four more sentences that use the missing words.**

1 Visit the museum ____________ learn about the city's history.
2 Go early ____________ it's free before 10:00 a.m.
3 Swim in the ocean ____________ take a boat trip.

B **Complete the rules with your answers from A.**

1 Use ____________ to give a reason.
2 Use ____________ to join two affirmative or two negative phrases.
3 Use ____________ to give a different idea.

C **Complete the sentences with *and*, *or*, or *because*.**

1 I go to two classes at the university: dance ____________ art. I like dance class ____________ the other students are fun.
2 Go to the bookstore ____________ buy a dictionary. Take your student ID card ____________ students get a 50% discount.
3 Do you like cold ____________ hot weather? I live near the beach ____________ I like hot weather.

D **Prepare a short blog and make recommendations for things to do in your city.**

1 Think about activities to do or places to go in the:
morning afternoon evening
2 Write sentences about your ideas using *and*, *or*, or *because*.
3 **IN PAIRS** Exchange your sentences and discuss your ideas. Do you like your partner's recommendations?

E **Write your short blog: *One Day in My City*.**

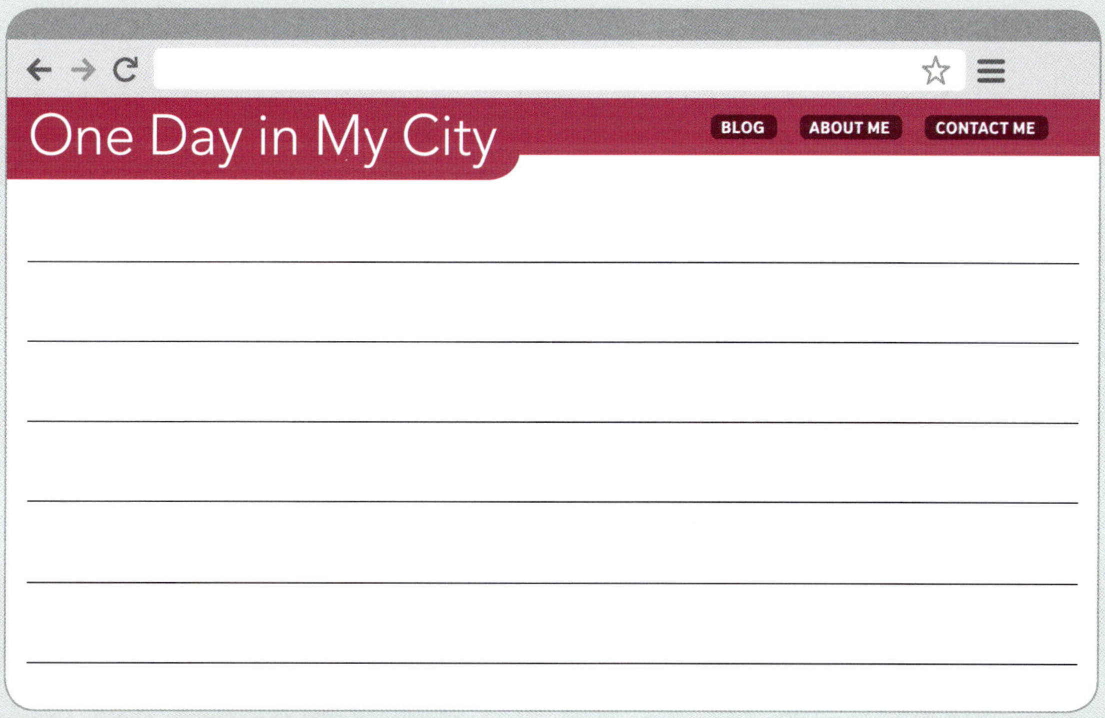

MAKE IT DIGITAL

Choose a city and search online for activities to do or places to go. Do you like the recommendations? What places are interesting?

VOCABULARY review

SCORE: / 5

A Match the sentence beginnings (1–5) to the sentence endings (a–e). Write the letter.

1 I can't do karate, ____
2 Can you dance salsa ____
3 I go to an art class ____
4 It's freezing today ____
5 It's rainy here, ____

a and it's snowy.
b because I want to draw pictures.
c but I can ride a horse.
d but it's warm.
e or play an instrument?

GRAMMAR review

SCORE: / 5

A Complete with *can* or *can't*.

1 ________ you ride a horse? No, I ________ .
2 I ________ ✓ drive a car, but I ________ ✗ ride a motorcycle.

B Complete the sentence with the words and the possessive *'s*.

These are ________ *(books/Jon)* and this is ________ *(phone/my friend)*.

C Complete the sentences.

1 I ________ a movie and Cindy ________ a cake.
2 We ________ dinner and we ________ to music.

6–10 correct: You can talk about free-time activities and what you can/can't do, learn about subjects, talk about weather, and describe what people are doing. You can use *can/can't*, possessive *'s* and present progressive statements.
0–5 correct: Look again at the Vocabulary and Grammar sections in the unit.

TOTAL SCORE: / 10

WHAT DO YOU KNOW NOW? Look back at page 45 and add the words you know now to the boxes.

STUDY SKILLS PRACTICING VOCABULARY

A IN PAIRS Do you agree (✓) or disagree (✗) with the sentences? Do you use other ways?

To practice vocabulary,
☐ I learn one new word every day.
☐ I play word games.
☐ I read English books and magazines.
☐ I talk to English speakers.
☐ I watch English movies and TV shows.

B 5.14 Look at the game. Listen to two players. Complete the rules with *left*, *letter* or *word*.

1 Move from ________ to right.
2 Choose a ________ and answer a question about it.
3 The answer is a ________ beginning with that letter.

C IN PAIRS Choose 15 words and write the questions. Then make your board. Use the same shapes from B.

D Play the game. One person asks questions. Then change roles.

UNIT 6 Health

WHAT DO YOU ALREADY KNOW?

1 Think about the places where you eat and what you eat there. Write words that you know in the boxes.

2 **IN PAIRS** Share and compare your information. Add more words to the boxes, if possible.

Food you like: ______________________
____
____
____

Food you don't like: ______________________
____
____
____

VIDEO

DISCUSS & SHARE

3 **IN GROUPS** Watch the video and answer the question.

SYM Eat in or eat out?

In this unit, you will ...

- describe people's appearance, talk about food and meals and ask and answer a quiz.
- use thinking skills: analyze, evaluate and predict.
- read two advertisements for food companies.
- use strategies to learn language to use when you need to think about your answer and agree or ask questions to continue a conversation.
- use communication skills to order food and drinks and write an online review.
- follow a food scientist to learn about their job and the skills needed to be in this industry.

LESSON 1 Appearance

VOCABULARY the face and body

A **IN PAIRS** Label the pictures with the words from your box. Then compare your answers.

Student A: eyes gray leg mouth nose old short slim

Student B: arm blond dark ears heavy tall teeth young

B **6.01 Listen and check. Then listen again and repeat.**

C **IN PAIRS Close your books. Point to your face/body and say the words. How many can you remember?**

PRONUNCIATION vowel sounds

A Match the words that have the same underlined sound.

arm dark heavy leg nose old

__________ , __________
__________ , __________
__________ , __________

MAKE IT YOURS

Use your dictionary to find more words to describe your face/body.

B **6.02 Listen and check your answers to A. Then listen again and repeat.**

LISTENING

A **6.03** Listen to the conversations and answer the question. Are the speakers talking about people in the same room or people in pictures?

Conversation 1: __________________

Conversation 2: __________________

B 6.03 LISTENING SKILL—Identify information **Listen again and label the people in the pictures with the phrases from the box.**

a Alison's brother	**b** Alison's father	**c** Alison's mother	**d** Alison's mother's sister
e Alison's mother's friend	**f** John	**g** Rosa's grandmother	**h** Rosa's grandmother's brother

Scene 1 (Conversation 1)

1 ______ 3 ______ 5 ______
2 ______ 4 ______ 6 ______

Scene 2 (Conversation 2)

1 ______
2 ______

C IN GROUPS THINKING SKILL—Analyze **Look at your group and answer the questions. Who has similar hair? Who has the same eye color? Who is tall and who is short?**

GRAMMAR *have*

A 6.04 Listen to the sentences from LISTENING **A** on page 56 and complete with ***has/have*** or ***don't/doesn't have***.

1 She ______ short brown hair.
2 They ______ the same color eyes.
3 We ______ the same nose.
4 I ______ a big nose.

B **Complete the table with your answers from A.**

Pronoun	**+**	**–**	**(Adjective +) Noun**
I/We/They	**1**	**3**	blond hair. big ears. blue eyes.
He/She	**2**	**4**	a small nose.

For more practice, go to page 78.

C IN PAIRS **Discuss. Look at the pictures in LISTENING B. Describe the people and say what they have / don't have.**

SPEAKING

A IN PAIRS Guess the person. Use the Confident Communicator box to help you.

Student A: go to page 69 of the Activity Bank. Student B: go to page 68 of the Activity Bank.

CONFIDENT COMMUNICATOR
KEEP TALKING

To think about your answer and continue the conversation, say:

Let me see … Does she have blue eyes?
Let me think … Is her name Lisa?

LESSON 2 Food

VOCABULARY food

A Write the words under the pictures. Some pictures have more than one word and one word is not used.

cereal chicken coffee ×2 eggs fish juice ×2
pasta salad ×2 sandwiches tea toast ×2 vegetables ×2

1 

____

2 

____

3 

____

4 

____

5 

____

6 

____

B 6.05 **Listen, check your answers to A and repeat.**

C IN PAIRS **Discuss. Tell your partner what you usually eat and drink for breakfast, lunch and dinner.**

READING

A **6.06 READING SKILL—Recognize different text types** Quickly read the texts. Which text is a blog and which is an advertisement?

COOK KING *The King of Dinners*

Help! I'm busy! I don't have any time to cook! Can you help?
Sure. We cook and bring delicious dinners to your home.

What do you mean? How does Cook King work?
Go to our website and order some meals. We cook your meal. Our driver drives to your house with your meal. You pay the driver.

Are there any vegetarian meals?
Yes! We have meals for everyone. We have some salads, some pasta with vegetables and other vegetable meals.

Do you cook and deliver at any time?
We open at 12:00 p.m. and close at 11:00 p.m.
We do not deliver after 11:00 p.m.

We don't have any cash!
No problem. Pay the driver with your credit card or debit card.

CONTACT COOK KING TODAY!

Time for Breakfast!

By: Michael White Mar. 15, 2019

Breakfast is my favorite meal of the day and it's important for our bodies. It prepares us for the day. Try these two meals for breakfast.

1 Cereal and toast—easy! You need some milk, some cereal and some bread. Don't forget to drink something. Drink a cup of coffee or a glass of orange juice.

2 Pancakes are another quick and easy meal. I like eating pancakes for breakfast, but some people eat them for a snack.

You need an egg, some milk and some flour. Mix everything together. Then cook.

B Read the texts in A again. Choose *T* (True) or *F* (False).

1 Cook King is a food business. T / F
2 It sells some vegetarian meals. T / F
3 Michael eats two meals for breakfast. T / F
4 Michael uses some milk for both meals. T / F

C IN GROUPS THINKING SKILL—Evaluate Do you have food businesses, like Cook King, in your city/town? Do you use them? Compare your answers.

GRAMMAR *some and any*

A Look at the advertisement in READING **A**. Find and circle three examples of ***any*** and three examples of ***some***. Then complete the rules.

1 Use *any* in affirmative sentences / negative sentences and questions.
2 Use *some* in affirmative sentences / negative sentences / questions.

For more practice, go to page 78.

B Underline examples of *a/an/some* + noun in the texts in READING A. Then complete the sentences below.

1 Use *a* or *an* for one thing / two or more things.
2 Use *some* to say there are / aren't two or more things.
3 Use *some* to say we do / do not know the exact number.

MAKE IT YOURS

Make a shopping list for some food or write an easy recipe for your favorite meal. Use your dictionary to help you.

C Complete the conversations with *some* or *any*.

Conversation 1
A: There isn't ___*any*___ cereal. There's ______ bread.
B: Great. Let's have ______ toast.

Conversation 2
A: Are there ______ vegetables?
B: No. There aren't ______ vegetables. There's ______ pasta.

D IN PAIRS Take turns to read the conversations in C.

SPEAKING

A IN PAIRS Read your list of food. Work together to make a meal for breakfast, lunch and dinner.

Student A

cake, cereal, coffee, eggs, fish, flour, salad, sandwiches

Student B

honey, juice, milk, pasta, chicken, tea, toast, vegetables

Student A: Let's make eggs on toast for breakfast. Are there any eggs on our list?
Student B: Yes. Do you have any toast?
Student A: Yes!

CONFIDENT COMMUNICATOR
KEEP TALKING

To continue the conversation, agree with your partner or ask about another meal.
Let's make eggs on toast. *OK! / I don't like eggs. How about cereal?*

LESSON 3 Feelings

VOCABULARY feelings

A Write the words from the box under the pictures (a–f). Then complete the sentences (1–6).

bored	excited	happy	hungry	sad	tired

a  ____________

b  ____________

c  ____________

d  ____________

e  ____________

f  ____________

1 I'm ____________ because it's sunny today.
2 There isn't any food and I'm ____________ .
3 I'm ____________ . This movie is terrible.
4 What a long day! I'm ____________ .
5 The party is tonight! I'm very ____________ !
6 Are you OK? You look very ____________ .

B 6.07 **Listen and check your answers to A. Then listen again and repeat.**

C **Write the adjectives from A in the correct group.**

Positive: ____________

Negative: ____________

D IN PAIRS **Discuss. How do you feel today?**

MAKE IT REAL

You may hear people adding *so*, *very* or *really* before adjectives to make them sound stronger.

*I'm **so** excited!* *I'm **very** sad.*
*I'm **really** bored.*

LISTENING

A IN PAIRS THINKING SKILL—Predict Look at the title of a book. Answer the questions.

1 What do you think it's about?
2 Who's the writer?
3 Do you think it's a popular book?

B 6.08 LISTENING SKILL—Identify information in an introduction
Listen to the introduction and check your ideas.

C 6.09 **Listen to the complete interview. Choose the correct words.**

1 Maria's grandfather is from America / Spain.
2 Her brother is always happy / tired.
3 Her father and grandfather are wearing dress hats / suits.
4 Maria and her brother are bored or hungry / sad.
5 Maria's parents are standing in front of / next to their house.
6 She lives in a beautiful and modern / old apartment.

D 6.09 **Listen again and write words related to the topics.**

1 family: *grandfather,* ____________
2 appearance: *tall, slim,* ____________
3 weather: *sunny,* ____________
4 the home: *apartment, big,* ____________
5 hobbies: *go for a walk,* ____________

GRAMMAR review

A Look at the sentences in the box from LISTENING **B**. Complete the table.

He's **always** tired.
We **don't have** blond hair.
I **can** drive a car.
I **live** in an apartment.
Their house is **next to** the restaurant.
We **aren't** smiling in the picture.
We **aren't** tall and slim.
~~We're short and heavy.~~

to be (+)	He's from Spain.	*We're short and heavy.*
to be (–)	My grandfather isn't from America.	**4**
simple present	He starts work at 8:00 a.m.	**5**
adverbs of frequency	He rarely has any free time.	**6**
to have (+)	They have dark hair!	
to have (–)	**1**	
present progressive (+)	He's dancing and laughing.	
present progressive (–)	**2**	
prepositions of place	They're standing in front of it.	**7**
can	**3**	

B Match the sentences from the table in A to the correct use. Write the numbers.

describe an ability or skill ______
describe someone's appearance ______ , ______
explain where something is ______
make general statements about your life ______
make very simple statements about yourself ______
say how often you do or don't do an activity ______
say what you are doing now ______

For more practice, go to page 79.

C IN PAIRS Complete the sentences in a quiz.

Student A: go to page 68 of the Activity Bank and complete the questions.
Student B: go to page 68 of the Activity Bank and complete the answers.

D 6.10 Compare and check the quiz. Then listen and check.

SPEAKING

A IN PAIRS Write two more questions for the quiz in GRAMMAR **C**. Then ask and answer the two new questions.

B As a class, use the quiz to ask one question to each student. Use the Confident Communicator box to help you.

C Share the answers with the class.

CONFIDENT COMMUNICATOR
KEEP TALKING

To continue the conversation, ask for more information:
Really? How old is your grandfather?
That's interesting! Tell me more about your job.

Language and Life

Communication – Cafe

FUNCTIONAL LANGUAGE order food and drinks

A Quickly read the conversation. Are the people in a coffee shop or a restaurant?

Waiter: Good morning. **What can I get you?**
Customer: Good morning. **Can I get a black coffee, please?**
Waiter: Sure. **What size: small, medium or large?**
Customer: **Large, please.** I'm very tired today!
Waiter: OK. **Any other drinks?**
Customer: Yes. **An orange juice, please.**
Waiter: No problem. One large black coffee and one orange juice. **Is that for here or to go?**
Customer: **Here, please.**
Waiter: **Can I get you some food?** We have some cookies and some cakes. The chocolate cake is delicious!
Customer: **No, thanks. That's all.**
Waiter: No worries. **That's $6.25, please.**
Customer: Here you go.
Waiter: Thank you. **Here's your change:** $0.75.

B **Match the conversation with the correct picture. Then write the price.**

1

2

Picture: ____________
$ ____________

C **Complete the table with the bold questions and answers from the conversation in A.**

Waiter	Customer
What can I get you?	Can I get a black coffee, please?
What size: small, medium or large?	Large, please.
Any other drinks?	An orange juice, please.
1 ______________________	**5** ______________________
2 ______________________	**6** ______________________
3 ______________________	
4 ______________________	

D 6.11 **Complete the conversation. Then listen and check.**

A: Hi, what can I ____________ you?
B: ____________ I have a coffee, please?
A: Sure. What ____________: small, medium or large?
B: Small, ____________ .
A: OK. Is that for ____________ or to go?
B: To ____________ , please.

E IN PAIRS **Practice the conversation in D. Change the drink and the size.**

WRITING an online review

A Quickly read the posts. Then choose the correct option.

1 The Blue Café is asking customers to **visit** / **vote for** the café.
2 There is a competition for **cakes** / **coffee shops**.
3 Meg is a **customer** / **waitress** at The Blue Café.

The Blue Café
Followers

BC **Dear customer,**
Thank you for visiting The Blue Café! Do you like our ☕? Does our homemade 🍰 make you 🙂? Yes? Please vote for us in the city's ***Top Coffee Shop*** competition! The link is below. ⬇ Please say why you like The Blue Café. Thank you! ❤

Top Coffee Shop competition

Meg ★★★★★ April 16 2019
The Blue Café is my favorite coffee ❶shop, The ❷Waiters are always happy ❸**but** friendly. The coffee ❹**great is**. It has some delicious cakes. There are ❺**any** salads and vegetarian meals. It's popular with students ❻**becuase** students have a 50% discount on Mondays!

B Look at the bold errors in Meg's post in A. Match each error to an error type.

capital letter = ____________
incorrect words (2) = ____________
punctuation = ___1___
spelling = ____________
word order = ____________

C Prepare a post for the competition.

1 Choose a coffee shop you like.
2 Make notes on:
- the people who work there
- the food and drinks you like
- the meals and food
- who likes the coffee shop and why

3 **IN PAIRS** Exchange your sentences and check for errors.

D Write your post.

MAKE IT DIGITAL

Look on social media for local coffee shops or other places in your city. Do you like their social media page? Send them a message!

VOCABULARY review

SCORE: / 5

A Circle the word that is different in each group. Then add one more word to each group.

1	ears	nose	tall	________
2	heavy	slim	tea	________
3	coffee	juice	mouth	________
4	excited	pasta	vegetables	________
5	bored	happy	sandwich	________

GRAMMAR review

SCORE: / 5

A Complete the sentences.

1 I ________ ✓ dark hair, but my two brothers ________ ✓ blond hair.

2 My mom ________ ✓ a small nose. She ________ ✗ a big nose.

3 There's ________ bread, but there aren't ________ eggs.

4 Sorry. There isn't ________ coffee. Do you want ________ juice?

5 I'm making ________ sandwiches and ________ pasta.

6–10 correct: You can talk about your appearance, people's appearance, food and meals, and feelings. You can use *have* and *some* and *any*.
0–5 correct: Look again at the Vocabulary and Grammar sections in the unit.

TOTAL SCORE: / 10

WHAT DO YOU KNOW NOW? Look back at page 55 and add the words you know now to the boxes.

FOLLOW A PRO FOOD SCIENTIST

A 6.12 Listen to a conversation with a food scientist. Who does he work for?

a university   a laboratory   a company

B **6.12 Listen again and complete the summary about Dr. Smith's job.**

Dr. Smith works for a ________. Dr. Smith gives ________ about food. Customers eat the food and choose their ________ sandwiches. The company ________ and ________ the sandwiches.

C **IN GROUPS Discuss.**

1 Is Dr. Smith's job important?
2 Is healthy food popular in your city/country?
3 What other jobs are there in the food industry?

UNIT 2 Lesson 1, page 17

SPEAKING Student A

A IN PAIRS Role-play

You are Alex Green.

Name	*Alex Green*
Home	*Mexico—small and quiet apartment*
Age	*24*
Email	*agreen98@emailforme.com*

UNIT 2 Lesson 3, page 20

READING

A IN PAIRS Look at the pictures. Find three differences.

1

2

UNIT 2 Lesson 3, page 21

SPEAKING Student A

A IN PAIRS Look at the picture. Make notes on the items in the room.

UNIT 2 Language and Life, page 22

FUNCTIONAL LANGUAGE Student A

E IN PAIRS Repeat the conversation from A with new information.

Hotel worker
There's a double room ($200) and a single room ($120).

Hotel guest
(Use your name and email.)
You want a double room for Saturday night.

UNIT 4 Lesson 1, page 37

SPEAKING Student A

E IN PAIRS Read the information about the tour. Take turns to answer the questions from Grammar A.

Boat tour
Start at: Green Park *Finish at:* West End
Visits: different places on the river
First tour: 10:00 a.m. *Last tour:* 6:00 p.m.
Tickets: buy on boat—$10 adults, $5 children and students

UNIT 5 Lesson 3, page 51

SPEAKING Student B

A IN GROUPS Role-play. What activities are you doing/not doing?

Name: James
Location: London Weather: rainy, cold
Activities: + reading a book, - practicing the piano

Activity Bank

UNIT 2 Lesson 1, page 17

SPEAKING Student B

A IN PAIRS Role-play

You are Jo Black.

Name	*Jo Black*
Home	*Brazil—big and noisy house*
Age	*26*
Email	*joblack@abcmail.co.br*

UNIT 3 Lesson 2, page 28

VOCABULARY Student B

A Take turns to read your text. (Do not show your partner the text.) Listen to your partner and complete your text.

I go to work by bus **1** ____________ the morning. I start work **2** ____________ 7:00 a.m. I work in an office. I go to college **3** ____________ Wednesday and **4** ____________ Thursday. The class is in the evening. It starts at 6:00 p.m. and ends at 8:00 p.m. I study on the weekend.

UNIT 4 Lesson 2, page 39

SPEAKING Student B

A IN PAIRS Look at the map and ask for directions.

Student A: ask for directions to the library.
Student B: ask for directions to the train station.

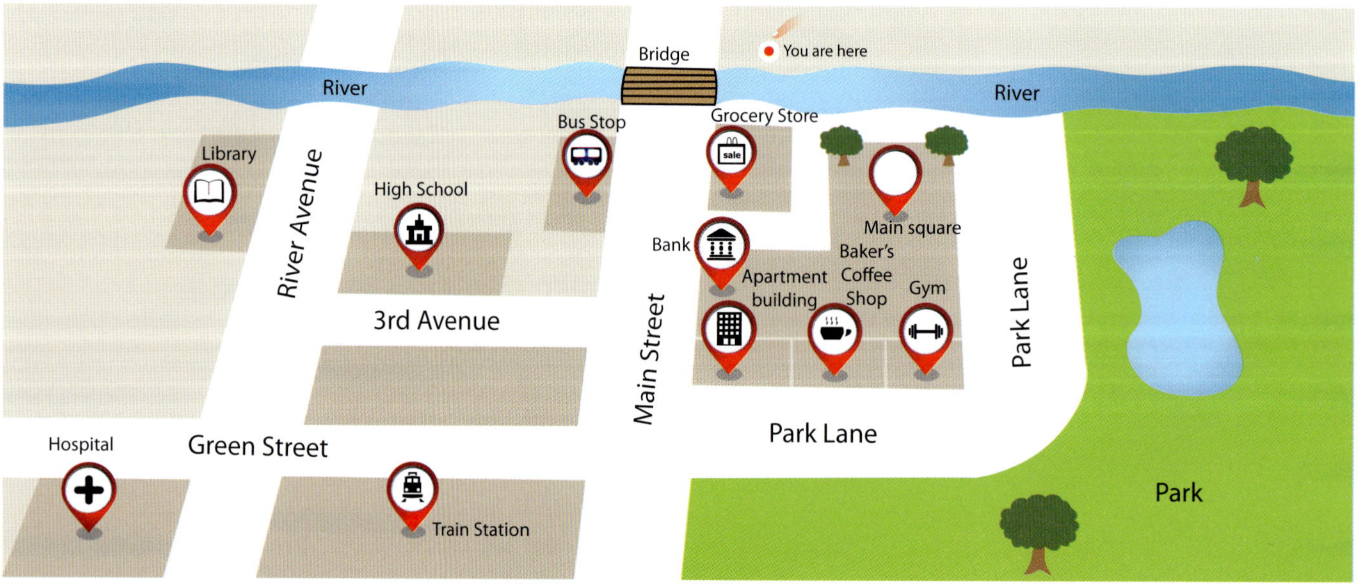

UNIT 2 Lesson 3, page 21

SPEAKING Student B

A IN PAIRS Look at the picture. Make notes on the items in the room.

UNIT 2 Language and Life, page 22

FUNCTIONAL LANGUAGE Student B

E IN PAIRS Repeat the conversation from A with new information.

<u>Hotel worker</u>
There's a double room ($150) and a single room ($90).

<u>Hotel guest</u>
(Use your name and email.)
You want a single room for Wednesday night.

Activity Bank

UNIT 4 Lesson 1, page 37

SPEAKING Student B

E IN PAIRS **Read the information about the tour. Take turns to answer the questions from Grammar A.**

Walking tour

Start at: the museum

Finish at: The Red Diner

Visits: different places in the city

First tour: 12:00 p.m.

Last tour: 4:00 p.m.

Tickets: buy online—$5 adults, $2 children and students

UNIT 4 Lesson 3, page 40

VOCABULARY

B 4.06 **Look at the pictures and match the opposites. Then listen, check and repeat.**

1 loose

5 tight

2 dressy

6 expensive

3 long

7 casual

4 cheap

8 short

UNIT 5 Lesson 3, page 51

SPEAKING Student C

A IN GROUPS **Role-play. What activities are you doing/not doing?**

Name: Isabel

Location: Mexico City Weather: cool, cloudy

Activities: + watching a movie, - sleeping

UNIT 5 Lesson 2, page 48

VOCABULARY Student A

D **Student A: read the name of the classroom items to Student B. Try to match each item to a subject.**

1 shoes

____

2 dictionary

____

3 paint brush

____

4 guitar

____

5 notebook and pens

____

6 safety glasses

____

7 calculator

____

Activity Bank

UNIT 5 Lesson 3, page 51

SPEAKING Student D

A IN GROUPS **Role-play. What activities are you doing/not doing?**

Name: Vincent
Location: Australia **Weather:** hot, sunny
Activities: + swimming, - meeting friends

UNIT 6 Lesson 1, page 57

SPEAKING Student B

A IN PAIRS **Guess the person.**

Look at the pictures of the people. Choose one person. Write their name. Do not tell your partner. Take turns to ask your partner questions to guess the person's name. Use short answers or long answers.

A: Is it a man? *B: No, he isn't.*
A: Is she tall? *B: Yes, she is tall.*

NINA

ALAN

FIONA

MAX

LISA

KRIS

RACHEL

BLAKE

UNIT 6 Lesson 3, page 61

GRAMMAR Student A

C **Complete the questions for the quiz.**

1. What *'s* your name?
2. ______ are you from?
3. Do you ______ a big family?
4. What color hair and eyes do you ______?
5. What do you ______?
6. Where ______ your college or workplace?
7. What time ______ you start and finish work or college?
8. What do you do ______ the weekend?
9. ______ you drive a car or ride a horse?
10. What ______ you doing now?

UNIT 6 Lesson 3, page 61

GRAMMAR Student B

C **Complete the answers for the quiz.**

1. *My* name's Louise Jones.
2. I'm from Argentina. ______ Argentinian.
3. I ______ three brothers, my parents and my grandfather. ______ 78 years old.
4. My hair ______ brown and I ______ blue eyes.
5. I'm ______ lawyer.
6. It's ______ Main Street. It's across ______ the park.
7. I get to work ______ 9:00 a.m. and I finish work at 5:00 p.m. I ______ home at about 6:00 p.m.
8. I usually meet my friends and ______ a movie.
9. I ______ drive a car, but I ______ ride a horse.
10. I'm ______ English and I'm talking to you!

Activity Bank

UNIT 4 Lesson 3, page 41

GRAMMAR

C Match the pictures (1–4) with the words from the box.

that these this those

UNIT 5 Lesson 2, page 49

SPEAKING Student A, B and C

Look at the lists below for one minute.
Student A: say one item.
Students B and C: guess the person's name.

A: apartment

B: It's Amanda's apartment.

Amanda	Irene
apartment	bag
jacket	car
paint brushes	laptop
phone	shoes

Simon	Victor
books	calculator
guitar	notebook
safety glasses	pens
watch	wallet

UNIT 5 Lesson 3, page 51

SPEAKING Student A

A IN GROUPS Role-play. What activities are you doing/not doing?

Name: Bianca
Location: Miami **Weather:** warm, sunny
Activities: + eating lunch, - studying

UNIT 6 Lesson 1, page 57

SPEAKING Student A

A IN PAIRS Guess the person.

Look at the pictures of the people. Choose one person. Write their name. Do not tell your partner. Take turns to ask your partner questions to guess the person's name. Use short answers or long answers.

A: Is it a man? *B: No, he isn't.*

A: Is she tall? *B: Yes, she is tall.*

Grammar Reference

UNIT 1 — *be* statements

Function

We use possessive adjectives to show possession *(e.g., My name …)* or express a connection with something *(e.g., My book …)* or someone (e.g., *My teacher …*). Use *be* statements to say your name.

Form

Possessive Adjectives		*To be* Affirmative	*To be* Negative	Object
My Your His/Her	name	is ('s)	is not (isn't)	Carlos.
Our Their	names	are	are not (aren't)	the same.

Use an apostrophe (') to make the contracted form, e.g., *is not = isn't.*

A Complete the *be* statements with the correct option.

1. Our names **are** / **is** the same.
2. Their family names **aren't** / **isn't** the same.
3. My name **is** / **are** Simon.
4. Her name **isn't** / **aren't** Ana.

B Complete the *be* statements with the correct form.

1. My name ______________ (–) Roger.
2. Her name ______________ (+) Liza.
3. Our names ______________ (–) the same.
4. Their names ______________ (+) the same.

UNIT 1 — subject pronouns and *be* statements

Function

We use subject pronouns as the subject of a sentence. Use *be* statements to give basic information about yourself.

Form

Subject Pronouns	*To be* Affirmative	*To be* Negative	
I	am / 'm	am not / 'm not	Spanish. / from Spain.
You	are / 're	are not / aren't	
He/She	is / 's	is not / isn't	
We/They	are	are not / aren't	

A Write the subject pronoun and the contracted form of *to be*.

1. You are from Mexico. ______________ from Mexico.
2. He is not British. ______________ British.
3. We are from Japan. ______________ from Japan.
4. They are Chinese. ______________ Chinese.

B Circle the error in each *to be* statement. Then write the correct word.

1. We're from France. We isn't from Spain. ______________
2. He isn't Chinese. He are Japanese. ______________
3. I'm from the US. I aren't from Canada. ______________
4. They aren't Spanish. They's Mexican. ______________

UNIT 1 — *yes/no* questions with *be*

Function

We use *yes/no* questions with *be* to ask basic questions and to receive short *yes/no* answers.

Form

Question			Answer		
To be	**Pronoun**	**Object**	***Yes/no***	**Pronoun**	***To be***
Am	I	your classmate?	Yes,	I	am.
			No,		am not / 'm not.
Is	she	your mother?	Yes,	she	is.
	he	your brother?	No,	he	is not / isn't.
Are	we	your friends?	Yes,	we	are.
	they		No,	they	are not / aren't.
	you	his grandparents?	Yes,	you	are.
			No,		are not / aren't.

A Choose the correct word to complete the *yes/no* questions with *be*.

1 **Is** / **Are** she your sister?
2 Are **they** / **she** your parents?
3 **Is** / **Are** we friends?
4 Is **he** / **they** your father?

B Complete the answers to the questions in A.

1 No, she ______________ .
2 No, they ______________ .
3 Yes, we ______________ .
4 Yes, he ______________ .

UNIT 2 — *be* information questions

Function

We use *be* information questions to ask basic questions. Use *How old* to ask about age. Use *What* to ask about a thing or a number. Use *Where* to ask about a place. Use *Who* to ask about a person or people.

Form

Question Word	*To be*	Subject
How old	are	your parents?
What	is	your email?
Where	are	they from?
Who	is	he/she?
How	are	you?

A Choose the correct word to complete the *be* information questions.

1 What **is** / **are** his name?
2 Where **is** / **are** they from?
3 How old **is** / **are** your sister?
4 How **is** / **are** you?

B Match the questions from A (1–4) to the answers (a–f). There are two answers you don't need.

1 What **is** / **are** his name? _____
2 Where **is** / **are** they from? _____
3 How old **is** / **are** your sister? _____
4 How **is** / **are** you? _____

a He's fine, thanks.
b They're 16.
c His name is Louis.
d They're from Canada.
e I'm fine, thanks.
f She's 17.

UNIT 2 — *a*/*an* singular and plural nouns

Function

We use *a*/*an* + singular noun to say there is one of something. Use plural noun + *–s* to say there are two or more of something.

Form

For one item:	**Example**
a + singular noun	a *laptop*
an + singular noun beginning with a vowel sound *(a, e, i, o, u)*	an *ID card*

For two or more items:	**Example**
number + noun + s	2 wallets
number + noun ending with *–ch* and *–sh* + *–es*	3 sandwiches

A Match the words.

1 an _____
2 a _____
3 two _____

a umbrella
b notebooks
c pen

B Circle the error. Then write *a*, *an* or the correct noun.

1 a ID card _______________
2 three bag _______________
3 an laptop _______________
4 two watchs _______________

UNIT 2 — *There is / There are*

Function

We use *There is* / *There are* to talk about one or more things.

Form

For two or more things:			
There	***are***	**Number**	**Plural Noun**
There	are	two four	bags. sandwiches.

For one thing:			
There	***is***	***a/an***	**Singular Noun**
There	is ('s)	a	pen.
		an	umbrella.

A Put the words in the correct order to make sentences.

1 five / are / bags. / There _______________.
2 is / a / There / chair. _______________.
3 umbrellas. / are / two / There _______________.
4 one / is / There / student. _______________.

B Complete the sentences with *is* or *are*.

1 There ___________ one bed next to the door.
2 There ___________ eight students.
3 There ___________ a desk in front of the window.
4 There ___________ two laptops on the desk.

UNIT 3 — simple present statements

Function

We use simple present statements to talk about what is and isn't true.

Form

Affirmative		
Subject Pronouns	**Verb**	
I You We They	go	to college.
	like	my job.
He She It	likes	his/her job.
	goes*	to work by bus.
	speaks	three languages.
Add *–s* to regular verbs. *Add *–es* to irregular verbs ending with *–o*.		

Negative		
Subject Pronouns	**Verb**	
I You We They	don't work	in a coffee shop.
He She It	doesn't speak	Spanish.

A Choose the correct word to complete the simple present statements.

1 I **work** / **works** in a restaurant.
2 He **live** / **lives** in Los Angeles.
3 Paul **speak** / **speaks** two languages.
4 They **don't** / **doesn't** go to college.

B Complete with the correct form of the verbs in parentheses.

1 I ___________ in the city. *(not live)*
2 He ___________ to college. *(go)*
3 They ___________ Spanish and English. *(speak)*
4 My brother ___________ . *(not work)*

UNIT 3 — *yes/no* questions with simple present

Function

We use *yes/no* questions with the simple present to ask basic questions about what is true. Use short answers to say what is and isn't true.

Form

***Yes/no* Questions with Simple Present**		
Do	you/we/they	work on Saturday?
Does	he/she/it	speak Chinese?

Short Answers					
Affirmative			**Negative**		
Yes,	I/you/we/they	do.	No,	I/you/we/they	don't.
	he/she/it	does.		he/she/it	doesn't.

A Complete the *yes/no* questions with simple present with *Do* or *Does*.

1 __________ they go to college?
2 __________ Angela study in the evening?
3 __________ you like your job?
4 __________ the coffee shop open on Sunday?

B Complete the short answers with *don't* or *doesn't*. Then match to the questions in A.

1 Yes, she __________ .
2 No, they __________ .
3 No, it __________ .
4 Yes, I __________ .

UNIT 3 — adverbs of frequency

Function

We use adverbs of frequency to talk about how regularly (%) something happens.

Form

Subject	*to be*	Adverb of Frequency	
The store	is	always	open.
They	are	usually	late.

Subject	Adverb of Frequency	Other Verbs	
I	often	have	breakfast at 7 a.m.
My parents	sometimes	stay	at the hotel.
We	rarely	go	by bus.
He	never	drinks	coffee.

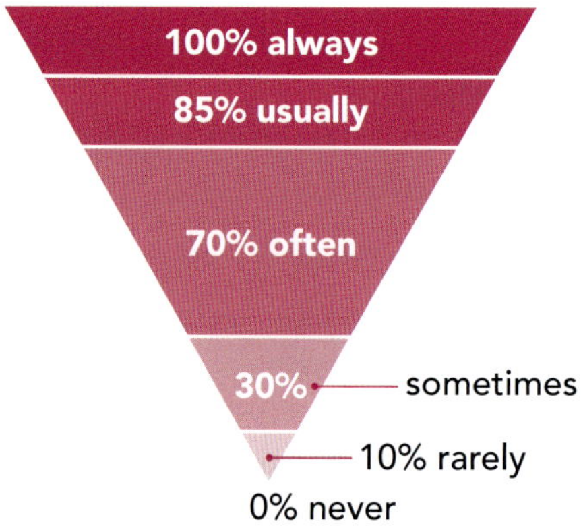

A Put the words in the correct order to make sentences.

1 sometimes / on / He / Saturday. / works

____

2 busy / The / usually. / is / college

____

3 at / breakfast / She / eats / 8 a.m. / often

____

4 are / waiters / friendly. / always / The

____

B Choose the correct adverb of frequency for the percentage in parentheses.

1 They **sometimes** / **usually** study in the evening. *(85%)*
2 The lessons are **always** / **often** good. *(100%)*
3 I **never** / **rarely** get up early. *(10%)*
4 We **often** / **sometimes** eat dinner at the restaurant. *(70%)*

UNIT 4 — simple present information questions

Function

We use simple present information questions to ask for specific information about something. Use *Where* to ask about a place. Use *What* to ask about general information. Use *When* to ask about a time. Use *How much* to ask about a price.

Form

Question Word	*Do/does*	Subject	Infinitive
Where	does	the bus	go?
	do	I	sit?
What	does	the tour	visit?
When	does	the store	open?
How much	do	the sandwiches	cost?

Use *do* for *I/you/we/they*. Use *does* for *he/she/it*.

A Choose the correct word to complete the simple present information questions.

1 What **do** / **does** you do?
2 When **do** / **does** the class start?
3 How much **do** / **does** a coffee cost?
4 Where **do** / **does** you live?

B Complete the simple present information questions with the correct question word.

1 ______________ do tourists buy tickets? The bus station.
2 ______________ does the store sell? Clothes and shoes.
3 ______________ does the suit cost? $200.
4 ______________ do you eat lunch? At 1 p.m.

UNIT 4 — imperatives

Function

We use imperatives to give directions to a specific place. Use simple present questions or *to be* questions to ask for directions and use *to be* statements to finish directions.

Form

Ask for Directions			
Question Word	**Verb**	**Object**	
Where	is	the park?	–
–	Is	the bus station	near here?

Give Directions	
Verb	**Directions**
Go	straight up Main Street.
Take	the first left.

Finish Directions		
Subject	**Verb**	**Directions**
It	is ('s)	next to the college.
The hotel		on the right.

A Match to make questions and statements about directions.

1 Is _____
2 It's _____
3 Where _____
4 Turn _____

a across from the train station.
b left and take the second right.
c the college near here?
d is the museum?

B Complete the sentences.

1 Excuse me, ______________ is the bookstore?
2 ______________ right and it's on the left.
3 ______________ straight up this road.
4 The ATM ______________ between the coffee shop and the bookstore.

UNIT 4 — *this/that/these/those*

Function

We use *this* and *these* to talk about objects that are very near to you. Use *that* and *those* to talk about objects that are not near to you.

Form

	This/that	**Singular Noun**
I like	this	jacket.
	that	T-shirt.

	These/those	**Plural Noun**
Do you like	these	boots?
	those	pants?

A Choose the correct word to complete the sentences.

1 This / These pants are very tight.
2 Look at that / those store across the street!
3 Do you like this / these shirt?
4 Are that / those boots new? They're nice!

B Circle the error. Write the correct word: *this, that, these* or *those*.

1 I don't like these bag by the window. ______________
2 Look at that red jeans over there! ______________
3 What color are this shoes? Blue or black? ______________
4 Those skirt is beautiful! I want it! ______________

UNIT 5 — *can/can't*

Function

We use *can/can't* to talk about activities that people are and aren't able to do.

Form

Questions			
Can	**Pronoun**	**Infinitive**	
Can	I/you/he/she/it/ we/they	play	the piano?

Statements		
Pronoun	***Can/can't***	**Infinitive**
I/You/He/She/It/ We/They	can	play football.
	can't	draw.

Short Answers		
Yes/no	**Pronoun**	***Can/can't***
Yes,	I/you/he/she/it/we/they	can.
No,		can't.

Use an apostrophe (') to make the contracted form, e.g., *cannot* = *can't*.

A Complete the statements with *can* or *can't*.

1 I can't speak French, but I ______________ speak Spanish.
2 Liz can ride a horse, but she ______________ ride a motorcycle.
3 They can draw animals, but they ______________ play the piano.
4 He can swim and he ______________ do karate.

B Complete the answers for the *Can* questions.

1 Can they dance salsa? Yes, ______________ .
2 Can Sara bake a cake? No, ______________
3 Can your brother ride a motorcycle? No, ______________ .
4 Can she speak two languages? Yes, ______________ .

UNIT 5 — possessive *'s*

Function

We use possessive *'s* to say that something belongs to a person.

Form

Name	's	Noun	
Jon	's	motorcycle	is very big.
Andy		books	are on the desk.

Singular Noun	's	Noun	
The teacher	's	jacket	is blue.

Name + *'s* + Noun
Jon's motorcycle is very big. Andy's books are on the desk.

Singular Noun + *'s* + Noun
The teacher's jacket is blue.

A Circle the examples of the possessive *'s* in the sentences.

1. Emily's books are in that bag.
2. My teacher's name is Pippa.
3. Jane's major is law.
4. Is that Roberto's laptop?

B Add the possessive *'s* to the sentences.

1. Is that Maria dictionary?
2. My sister bag is on the desk.
3. The teacher classes are interesting.
4. Where is Paola laptop?

UNIT 5 — present progressive statements

Function

We use the present progressive to talk about an activity that is happening now.

Form

Statements		
Pronoun	***To be* (+/-)**	**+ *–ing* (Regular Verbs)**
I	am ('m)	reading a book. watching a movie. eating.
	am ('m) not	
He/She/It	is ('s)	
	is not (isn't)	
You/We/They	are	
	are not (aren't)	

Pronoun	*To be* (+/-)	+ *–ing* (Irregular Verbs)	
		One Vowel and Final Consonant	**Verbs with a Final e**
I	am ('m) am ('m) not	getting coffee. swimming. shopping.	having fun. practicing English. writing.
He/She/It	is ('s) is not (isn't)		
You/ We/They	are are not (aren't)		

Spelling rules for irregular verbs:

- end of verb is consonant, vowel, consonant: double final consonant and add *–ing*
- final *–e*: delete final *–e* and add *–ing*

A Choose the correct words to complete the sentences.

1 We're practiceing / practicing English.
2 Bella's haveing / having fun in the park.
3 They're swiming / swimming in the sea.
4 I'm reading / readding a book.

B Complete the sentences with the correct present progressive form of the verb.

1 We ______________ sandwiches. (not eat)
2 I ______________ coffee with my friends. (have)
3 They ______________ in the city. (not shop)
4 He ______________ for an exam. (study)

UNIT 6 — *have*

Function

We use *have* to talk about someone's appearance or something that someone owns.

Form

Affirmative		
Pronoun	***Have***	**(Adjective +) Noun**
I/You/We/ They	have	dark hair. small ears. brown eyes.
He/She	has	a big nose.

Negative			
Pronoun	***Don't/doesn't***	***Have***	**(Adjective +) Noun**
I/You/We/ They	don't	have	dark hair. small ears. brown eyes.
He/She/It	doesn't		a big nose.

A Complete the sentences with *have* or *has*.

1 Rachel and Alissa ______________ blue eyes.
2 She ______________ a small nose.
3 Pietro doesn't ______________ big ears.
4 My brother and I ______________ blond hair.

B Circle the error in each sentence. Write the correct form of *have*.

1 My sister doesn't has brown hair. She has red hair. ______________
2 Dan's father have a big nose, but Dan has a small nose. ______________
3 They both has big eyes. They don't have big ears. ______________
4 We both have the same color hair, but you has short hair. ______________

UNIT 6 — *some* and *any*

Function

We use *some* to say what there is or what we have. Use *any* to say what is not there or what we don't have.

Form

Questions		
Is there	any	coffee?
Are there		vegetables?

Affirmative	
For one thing:	**Example**
a/an + singular noun	There's a cup of tea on the table. There's an egg.
For two or more things:	**Example**
some + plural noun	There are some pancakes. There are some vegetables.

Negative	
For two or more things:	**Example**
any + plural noun	There aren't any snacks. There aren't any sandwiches.

A Match to make questions or statements with *some* and *any*.

1 There's ___
2 There aren't ___
3 We have ___
4 Is there ___

a some sandwiches.
b any pasta?
c any eggs.
d a glass of orange juice.

B Complete the sentences with *an*, *any* or *some*.

1 Are there __________ tomatoes?
2 There's __________ bread on the table.
3 Let's make __________ pasta.
4 Do you have __________ egg?

UNIT 6 — review

Form

Grammar	Example
to be (+)	I'm from France. They're tall and heavy.
to *be* (–)	My friend isn't from this city. We aren't short and slim.
simple present	He gets up at 6 a.m. They don't live in the UK.
adverbs of frequency	He often draws animals on Sunday. The store is always open late.
to have (+)	I have blond hair. We have big eyes.
to have (–)	He doesn't have big ears. They don't have dark hair.
present progressive (+)	He's dancing to the music. We're reading a magazine.
present progressive (–)	I'm not cooking dinner. They aren't eating in a restaurant.
can/can't	I can ride a horse. He can't bake a cake.

A Complete the sentences with words from the box. There are two words you don't need.

always any are can have walk

1 My sister doesn't __________ blue eyes.
2 The students __________ practicing English.
3 I __________ to work on Mondays.
4 The course is __________ popular.

B Complete the questions with the correct verb.

1 When __________ you go to bed?
2 How much __________ the pizzas?
3 __________ you play the piano?
4 What color eyes do they __________ ?

Irregular Verbs

Infinitive	Simple past	Past participle
be	was/were	been
become	became	become
begin	began	begun
break	broke	broken
bring	brought	brought
build	built	built
buy	bought	bought
catch	caught	caught
choose	chose	chosen
come	came	come
cost	cost	cost
cut	cut	cut
do	did	done
draw	drew	drawn
drink	drank	drunk
drive	drove	driven
eat	ate	eaten
fall	fell	fallen
feed	fed	fed
feel	felt	felt
find	found	found
fly	flew	flown
get	got	gotten
give	gave	given
go	went	gone
grow	grew	grown
hang	hung	hung
have	had	had
hear	heard	heard
hit	hit	hit
hold	held	held
hurt	hurt	hurt
keep	kept	kept
know	knew	known
leave	left	left
let	let	let
lose	lost	lost
make	made	made
meet	met	met
pay	paid	paid
put	put	put
read	read	read
ride	rode	ridden
ring	rang	rung
rise	rose	risen
run	ran	run
say	said	said
see	saw	seen
sell	sold	sold
send	sent	sent
set	set	set
sing	sang	sung
sit	sat	sat
speak	spoke	spoken
stand	stood	stood
stick	stuck	stuck
take	took	taken
teach	taught	taught
tell	told	told
think	thought	thought
throw	threw	thrown
understand	understood	understood
wake	woke	woken
wear	wore	worn
win	won	won
write	wrote	written

Pronunciation Symbols

Vowels

ɪ	d**i**d
ɛ	b**e**d
æ	b**a**d
ʌ	c**u**p
ʊ	b**oo**k
ə	b**a**n**a**n**a**
i	f**ee**d
ɑ	f**a**ther, b**o**x
ɔ	t**a**ll
u	st**u**dent, f**oo**d
ɚ	sh**ir**t, b**ir**thday
eɪ	d**a**te, t**a**ble
aɪ	cr**y**, **eye**
ɔɪ	b**oy**
oʊ	c**o**mb, p**o**st
aʊ	ab**ou**t, h**ow**

Consonants

p	**p**ark, ha**pp**y
b	**b**ack, ho**bb**y
t	**t**ea
d	**d**ie
k	**c**ame, **k**itchen, **q**uarter
g	**g**ame, **g**o
f	**f**ace, **ph**otographer
V	**v**egetable
θ	**th**ing, ma**th**
ð	**th**en, **th**at
s	**c**ity, **s**ummer
z	plea**s**e, goe**s**
ʃ	**sh**e, **sh**op
ʒ	lei**s**ure
h	**h**ot, **wh**o
tʃ	**ch**icken, wa**tch**
dʒ	**j**acket, oran**g**e
m	**m**en
n	su**n**, **kn**ow
ŋ	su**ng**, si**ng**er
w	**w**eek, **wh**ite
r	**r**ain, **wr**iter
l	**l**ight, **l**ong
j	**y**es, **u**se, m**u**sic

RHONA SNELLING

SPEAK YOUR MIND

WORKBOOK
+ access to Audio

S
STARTER

macmillan education

Table of Contents

UNIT 1

Me

LESSON 1 Introductions

LISTENING

A 1.1 **Listen to the conversation. Are the people students or co-workers?** ______________

B 1.1 **Listen to the conversation and write the names.**

Francesca Max Mrs. Woman

______________ ______________ ______________

SKILLS

It is polite to learn a new person's name. It is the first stage of a new friendship.

C 1.1 **Listen to the conversation and number the sentences in the correct order.**

a ☐ I'm Francesca. Nice to meet you, Max.

b ☐ Good evening! Welcome to the first English class! I'm your teacher. My name's Mrs. Wood.

c ☐ Sorry? Can you repeat that?

d ☐ Francesca. Nice to meet you, too. Ah, here's the teacher.

e ☐ Hello, I'm Max. I'm here for the English class. What's your name?

f ☐ Francesca. Fran-ces-ca.

VOCABULARY

A Write the correct phrase from the box under each picture.

Good afternoon. Good evening. Good morning.

1 
____

2 
____

3 
____

B Complete the conversations with the correct words from the box.

fine Goodbye Hello How Nice See too

1 A: ______________, Amelia. ______________ are you?
B: I'm ______________, thanks.

2 A: ______________ you, Lenny!
B: ______________!

3 A: I'm Lorenzo. ______________ to meet you.
B: I'm Josh. Nice to meet you, ______________.

GRAMMAR

A Match the phrases to make sentences.

1 The word order for *be* statements _____
2 We use a possessive adjective _____
3 We join two words _____

a with an apostrophe.
b is subject—verb—object.
c before a noun.

B Circle the examples of the verb *to be*.

1 I'm Mr. Cooper.
2 My name's Andreas.
3 Her name is Irene.
4 Your name isn't Harry.
5 I'm fine, thanks.

C Unscramble and write the sentences.

1 name / My / Dora. / is ____________________
2 not / name / Charlotte. / Her / is ____________________
3 co-worker. / my / is / This ____________________
4 isn't / His / Tony. / name ____________________
5 Mr. / is / name / Banks. / Your ____________________

D Complete the pairs of sentences with the other correct form of *to be*.

1 I _____ Emily. = I'm Emily.
2 His name is Tom. = His name _____ Tom.
3 Her name __________ Karina. = Her name isn't Karina.
4 Your name __________ Tilda. = Your name's Tilda.
5 My name is not Gina. = My name __________ Gina.

E Complete the conversation with the correct words.

Tommy: Good afternoon. My name _____ Tommy. What _____ your name?
Luis: I _____ Luis. Nice to meet you, Timmy.
Tommy: My name __________ Tommy. My name __________ Timmy.
Luis: Sorry! Your name __________ Tommy. Nice to meet you.
Tommy: Nice to meet you, too. This __________ my co-worker. His name __________ Sebastian.
Luis: Nice to meet you, Sebastian.

READING

A Read the cards. Who is a student? Who is a worker?

Santiago: ______________ Ayako: ______________

University of São Paulo

Santiago Medina

Subject	Tourism
Name	Santiago Medina
Nationality	Mexico
First language	Spanish

STAFF Hospital São Paulo

Ayako Silva

Doctor

Japan

Japanese, Portuguese,

French, English

B Read the cards in A again and complete the sentences.

1 Santiago is from ______________. He's ______________. His first language is ______________.

2 Ayako is from ______________. She's ______________. Her first language is ______________. Her other languages are ______________, ______________, and ______________.

SKILLS

Read the sentence below and underline the country, nationality, and language.

Jonah is from the United States of America. He is American.
His first language is English.

VOCABULARY

A Write the countries under the flags.

1  ______________

2  ______________

3  ______________

4  ______________

B Unscramble and write the words.

1 thirbis ______________
2 hissnpa ______________
3 rnaceaim ______________
4 adcianna ______________
5 nilazbira ______________

C Complete the sentences with words from the box. There is one extra word you do not need.

British Canada Chinese French German Mexican

1 Anton is from France. He's ______________.
2 Elke is from Germany. Her first language is ______________.
3 Weiling is from China. She's ______________.
4 Justin is from ______________. His first language is English.
5 I'm from Mexico. I'm ______________.

GRAMMAR

A Match the words to their grammatical descriptions.

1 is not ____
2 's ____
3 she ____
4 I am ____

a subject pronoun
b to be (affirmative)
c to be (negative)
d apostrophe

B Read the first sentence and complete the second sentence with the correct subject pronoun from the box.

He She They We

1 Chao isn't from Japan. = ________________'s from China.
2 I'm from the US and Zac is from the US. = ________________'re from the US.
3 Jane is from the UK. = ________________'s from the UK.
4 Marco and Giulia are from Italy. = ________________'re from Italy.

C Unscramble and write the sentences.

1 are / from / the / not / US. / We ________________
2 Canada. / from / are / They ________________
3 is / from / He / Mexico. / not ________________
4 from / I / France. / am ________________
5 not / You / Germany. / from / are ________________

D 1.2 Listen and complete the sentences with words from the box.

'm not 'm 's aren't isn't (x2)

1 They *'re*________ from Japan. They ________ from China. Their first language ________ Chinese.
2 He ________ from Canada. He ________ from the UK. His first language is French.
3 My first language is Spanish. I ________ from Spain. I ________ from Mexico.

E Rewrite the sentences in C with the short form of *to be*.

1 ________________
2 ________________
3 ________________
4 ________________
5 ________________

LISTENING

A 1.3 Listen to Jeff talk about his family. Label the people in the pictures.

Benji Bill Jake Jenny Nancy Seth Tonya

B 1.3 Listen to Jeff talk about his family. Correct the sentences.

Seth and Nancy are Jeff's grandparents. Jeff's father is 49. Benji is Jeff's brother. Tonya is Jeff's wife. Jake is 27. Jenny is Jake's sister.

SKILLS

Key words give us important information. They help us understand more about a person or situation.
*Nina is my **sister**. She's **20** years old.*

VOCABULARY

A Complete the words with the correct letters.

1 da___g___te___
2 w___f___
3 m___t___er
4 g___an___mo___her
5 s___s___er

B Write the opposite words for the words in A.

1 ___son___
2 ______
3 ______
4 ______
5 ______

C Complete the sentences with the correct word.

1 This is my mom and dad. They are my ______.
2 This is my grandmother and my grandfather.
They are my ______.
3 My father's wife is my ______.
4 My mom's dad is my ______.
5 Mr. and Mrs. Black are ______ and wife.

GRAMMAR

A Choose the correct option to complete the sentences.

1 The correct word order for *yes/no* questions with *be* is
Pronoun—verb—object. / Verb—pronoun—object. / Object—pronoun—verb.

2 The correct word order for *yes/no* short answers is
Yes/No—verb—pronoun. / Pronoun—verb—*yes/no*. / *Yes/No*—pronoun—verb.

B Complete the questions with the correct form of the verb *to be* or the correct pronoun.

1 Are ______________ your friends?
2 ______________ he your co-worker?
3 Is ______________ your sister?
4 ______________ you his mom?

C Complete the short answers with the correct form of the verb *to be* from the box. There are two extra words you do not need.

am   am not   are   aren't   is   isn't

a Yes, I ______________.
b Yes, he ______________.
c No, they ______________.
d No, she ______________.

D Match the short answers in C to the questions in B.

1 ______________
2 ______________
3 ______________
4 ______________

E Read the conversation and complete the questions and short answers about Lara's family.

Tammy: ______________ Henry and Elsa your grandparents?

Lara: No, ______________ ______________. They're my parents.

Tammy: Oh, OK. ______________ Stacey your sister?

Lara: Yes, ______________ ______________. She's my sister and my best friend. She's great!

Tammy: My sister is great, too. ______________ Phil your brother?

Lara: No, ______________ ______________. Phil is my co-worker. Felix is my brother.

Tammy: ______________ Darlene and Emma your friends?

Lara: Yes, ______________ ______________. They're my friends from college.

Go to p. 125 for Progress Check.

Language and Life

Communication: Personal Information

FUNCTIONAL LANGUAGE

A Write the correct information from the box for each sentence.

email major name nationality phone number

1 Paola. My last name is Di Giulio. ____________________
2 Languages. ____________________
3 I'm Italian. ____________________
4 paola1999@me.com ____________________
5 My cell number is 555-281-0439. ____________________

B 1.4 Listen and complete the form.

Name		
Nationality		
Major		
Email		
Phone		

WRITING

A Read the sentences and circle the capital letters.

1 I'm Lexi. My last name is Sanders.
2 I'm from the UK. I'm British.
3 My first language is Spanish.
4 I speak English and Chinese.
5 This is my friend, Maliek.

B Rewrite the sentences correctly using capital letters.

1 i'm janey. i'm a student. ____________________
2 my first language is english. ____________________
3 his name is juan. ____________________
4 they are from mexico. they are mexican. ____________________
5 we aren't from the us. ____________________

UNIT 2 My Place

LESSON 1 Homes

LISTENING

A Look at the pictures. Write words from the box to describe the building and the room.

____
____

____
____

big modern old small

SKILLS

Look at the pictures and think about everything you can see—e.g., the people, location, and activity. This helps you to prepare and focus on the subject when you listen.

B 2.1 Listen and choose the correct option.

1 Speaker 1 talks about the place in picture 1 / 2.
2 Speaker 2 talks about the place in picture 1 / 2.

C 2.2 Listen and complete the descriptions.

Speaker 1
1 I like _______________ places.
2 This room is very _______________, and it's very old.
3 It isn't _______________.

Speaker 2
1 It's big and it's _______________.
2 This building isn't small or _______________.
3 It's _______________, and I love it!

VOCABULARY

A Complete the adjectives.

1 b_______________l
2 b_____g
3 m_______________n
4 n_______________y
5 o_____d
6 q_______________t
7 s_______________l
8 u_______________y

B Write the adjectives from A in the correct categories.

size: _____*big*_____ _______________
age: _______________ _______________
look: _____*ugly*_____ _______________
noise: _______________ _______________

C Complete the sentences with the correct adjective.

1 The house isn't _______________. It's noisy.
2 It isn't a modern apartment. It's _______________.
3 My room isn't _______________. It's big.
4 I think my place is beautiful. It isn't _______________!

GRAMMAR

A Choose the correct words to complete the rules.

1 The word order for *be* information questions is **Question word—*to be*—subject** / **Subject—question word—*to be***.
2 We use **the same** / **a different** question word to ask about different types of information.
3 We **use** / **do not use** a capital letter for the first letter of the question word.

B Match to make questions.

1 What ______ a your grandparents?
2 Where is ______ b are you?
3 Who ______ c are their names?
4 How ______ d is he?
5 How old are ______ e she from?

C Complete the *be* questions with *is* or *are*.

1 Where ______________ you from?
2 How old ______________ your brother?
3 What ______________ her name?
4 Who ______________ they?
5 How ______________ your parents?

D Complete the answers with *is* or *are*. Then match to the questions in C.

1 They ______________ fine, thanks. ______
2 Her name ______________ Katy. ______
3 I ______________ from the UK. ______
4 They ______________ my co-workers. ______
5 He ______________ 19. ______

E Read the conversation and complete the *be* questions and answers.

Benny
Online

Hi Benny, **1** ______________ are you? Are you free?

Hey, Mitchell! I **2** ______________ fine, thanks. I'm not free.

Why?

My family is here for coffee.

3 ______________'s there?

My mom and dad, my brother, and my grandfather.

Your grandfather? **4** ______________ ______________ is he?

He **5** ______________ 82.

Wow! **6** ______________ is his house?

It **7** ______________ downtown. It isn't a house. It's a small apartment.

8 ______________'s your brother's name?

His name **9** ______________ Casey. He's great. Come over and say hello!

OK, thanks!

LISTENING

A 2.3 Listen to the conversation and choose the correct words.

1 The speakers are **friends** / **family**.
2 The boy is at **school** / **home** and the woman is at **school** / **home**.
3 The speakers talk about a **bag** / **classroom**.

SKILLS

The first time we listen, think about the main idea. For example, *Who are the speakers? Where are they? What is the conversation about?*

B 2.3 Listen to the conversation. Number the objects in the correct order.

a laptop	1	**d** phone	☐	**g** umbrella	☐
b notebooks	☐	**e** sandwiches	☐	**h** wallet	☐
c pens	☐	**f** transit card	☐		

C 2.3 Listen to the conversation and choose *True* or *False*. Rewrite the false sentences correctly.

1 Nathan's bag is black. **True** / **False** ______________________
2 The laptop isn't in Nathan's bag. **True** / **False** ______________________
3 Three or four notebooks are in Nathan's bag. **True** / **False** ______________________
4 Nathan's phone isn't in the bag. **True** / **False** ______________________
5 Nathan's transit card is in the bag. **True** / **False** ______________________

VOCABULARY

A Complete the words with the correct letters.

a

1 ___ ___ card

b

2 ___ a ___ ___e ___

c

3 ph___ n ___

d

4 ___ a ___ ___o___

e

5 ___ e ___

f

6 ___ a ___ ___ ___

g

7 n ___ t ___ book

h
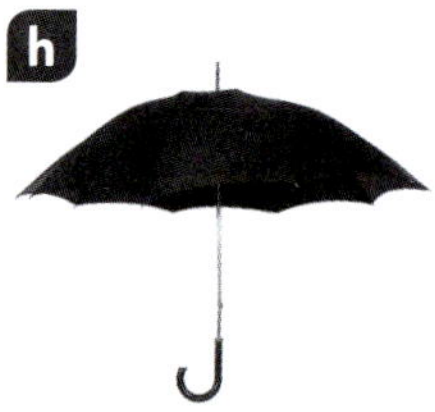
8 ___ mbr ___ ll ___

i

9 br___sh

j
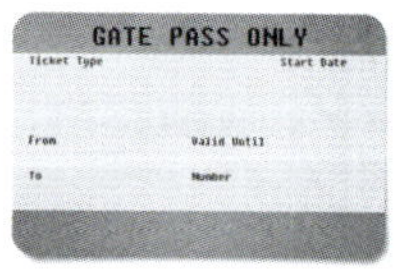

10 tr___ ns ___ t c ___

B 2.4 Write the words in A in the correct syllable groups. Then listen and check.

One: ______________________
Two: ______________________
Three: ______________________

C Complete the categories with words from A.

1 send an email: *phone* ______ ______
2 for your hair: ______
3 use for the bus: ______
4 use to look at the time: ______ ______ ______
5 use to put money in: ______
6 use to write on paper: ______

GRAMMAR

A Match to complete the rules.

1 We use *a* + noun ___
2 We use *an* + noun ___
3 We use number + noun ___
4 We use number + noun ___

a + *es* for plural nouns ending with *ch* and *sh*.
b + *s* for plural nouns.
c for singular nouns.
d for singular nouns beginning with a vowel sound.

B Complete the table with the nouns.

brush ID cards laptops notebook pen phones transit card umbrellas wallet watches

Singular nouns	Plural nouns

C Write *a* or *an*.

1 ___ notebook
2 ___ umbrella
3 ___ wallet
4 ___ ID card
5 ___ phone
6 ___ brush
7 ___ laptop
8 ___ transit card
9 ___ pen
10 ___ watch

D Write *s* or *es*.

1 three brush___
2 two umbrella___
3 two or three pen___
4 five notebook___
5 two wallet___
6 four phone___
7 ten watch___
8 six laptop___
9 five or six ID card___
10 four transit card___

E Read the two lists and correct the nine errors.

Remember to buy:
five new pens: two black pen and three blue pen
two or three notebookes
a ID card for college
an transit card for seven days
a wallet for Dad's birthday

My wish list
a new laptop for college
two brushs for my sister
an phone
two watchs—a watch for sports and a watch for going out
a umbrella for my vacation

VOCABULARY

A Look at the picture (a) and choose *True* or *False*. Rewrite the false sentences correctly.

1 The chair is in front of the desk. **True / False**

____

2 The lamp is on the desk. **True / False**

____

3 The bag is under the chair. **True / False**

____

4 The umbrella is next to the book. **True / False** _______________

5 The umbrella is between the book and the desk. **True / False** _______________

B Look at the picture (b) and complete the sentences.

1 The window is between the _______________ and the lamp.
2 The chair is _______________ the window.
3 The bed is next to the _______________.
4 The bag is _______________ the bed.
5 The _______________ are on the bed.
6 The door is _______________ the lamp.

READING

A Read the description. What is it about? Circle the best topic.

a classroom in a school | a room in a person's home | an office in a building

21. Oct 11:24

The room is very big. There are two windows—one is big and one is small. There's a desk and a chair in front of the big window. There are three books on the desk. There's a laptop and a phone on the desk. There are five notebooks. There are three or four pens on the notebooks. There's a bed between the windows. There are two bags under the bed. There's a closet next to the small window. There's an umbrella behind the closet.

SKILLS

Read a new text quickly (20 seconds) and identify the topic. Do not check the meaning of new words. Focus on the topic or general idea the first time you read the text.

B Read the description. Write the words in the correct place.

1 _______________

2 _______________

3 _______________

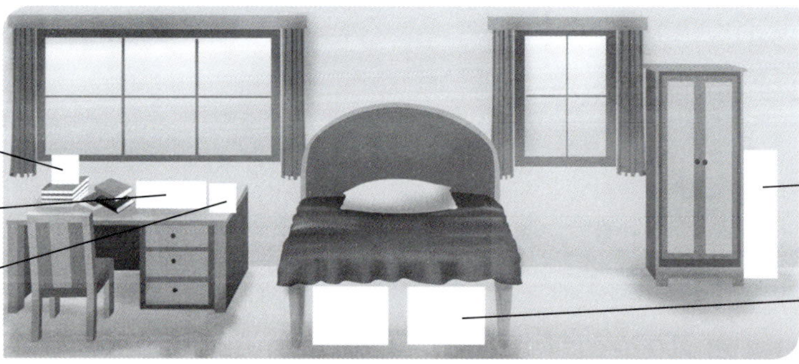

5 _______________

4 _______________

GRAMMAR

A Complete the rules with *is* or *are*.

1. We use *There* ______________ for one thing.
2. We use *There* ______________ for two things.
3. We use the contracted form *'s* for *There* ______________.

B Choose the correct word.

1. There **is** / **are** a bag on the desk.
2. There **is** / **are** two books under the bed.
3. There **is** / **are** a big closet next to the door.
4. There **is** / **are** two chairs in front of the window.
5. There **is** / **are** a lamp behind the door.

C Complete the sentences with *is, are, a,* or *an*.

1. There ______________ five rooms in the apartment.
2. There is ______________ umbrella on the desk.
3. There ______________ eight desks in the classroom.
4. There ______________ a phone in the bag.
5. There is ______________ watch on the bed.

D Correct the six errors in the description.

There is two bedrooms in the apartment. The big bedroom is beautiful. There is three big windows. There are a bed. There's a desk. There are two chairs.
The small bedroom isn't beautiful. There are a window. There's an bed behind the door. There are a small desk next to the bed.

E 2.5 Listen and complete the description.

There ____ in the apartment. The small room is my favorite. There ____.
There ____ behind the door.
There ____ next to the bed. There ____ under the bed.

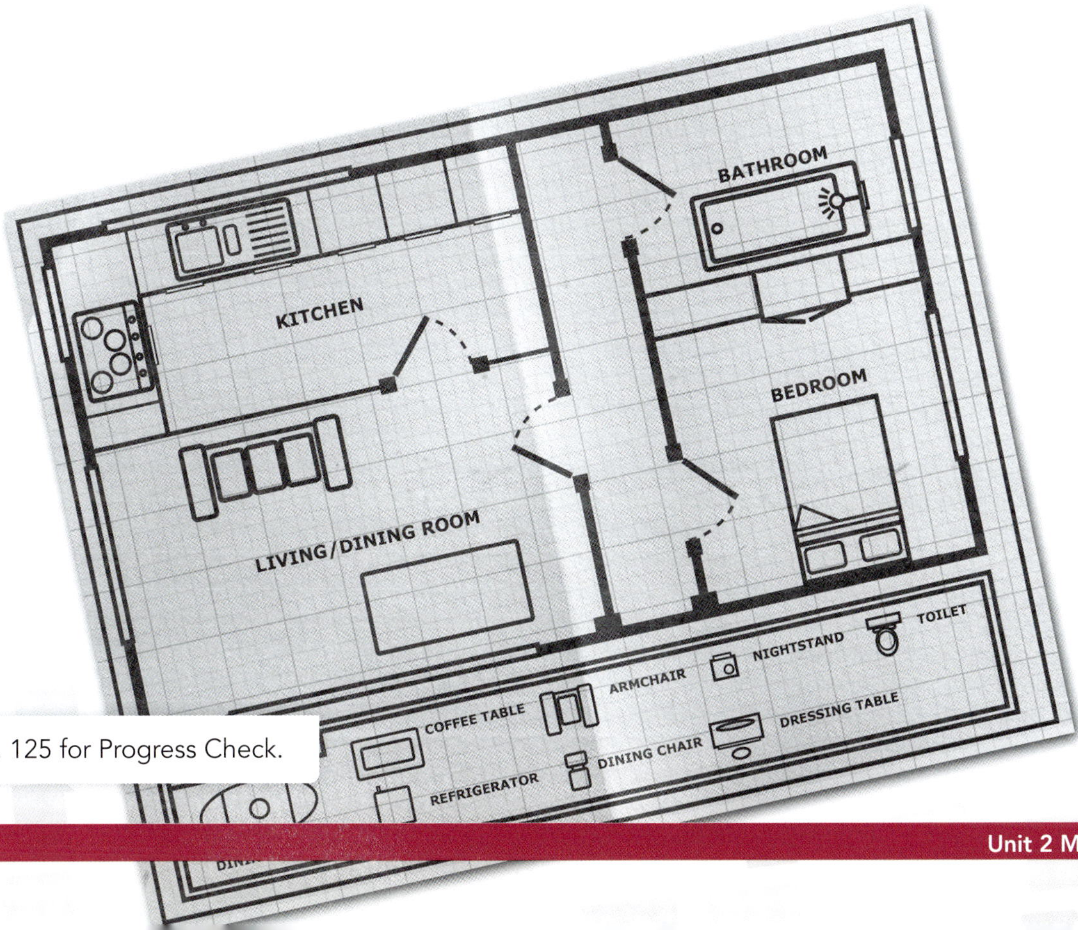

Go to p. 125 for Progress Check.

Language and Life

Communication: Hotel Room

FUNCTIONAL LANGUAGE

A **2.6 Listen and complete the conversation.**

Hotel worker: Park Hotel?
Kellie: Good afternoon. Yes, I want to **1** ______________ a double room for **2** ______________ night, please.
Hotel worker: OK. Let me see. Yes. There's a double room.
Kellie: Good. Thank you. **3** How ______________ is it?
Hotel worker: It's $175 and guests pay at the hotel, miss. Could you please give me your name and email?
Kellie: Can you **4** ______________ that, please?
Hotel worker: $175. **5** ______________ pay at the hotel; name and email?
Kellie: Kellie, K-E-L-L-I-E, Black, B-L-A-C-K. My email is kellieb1234@mymail.com.
Hotel worker: Thank you. That's one double room for Saturday.
Kellie: Thank you for your **6** ______________. Goodbye.
Hotel worker: You're welcome, have a good day! Goodbye.

B **2.7 Listen to the hotel worker and choose *Polite* or *Not polite*.**

1 Polite / Not polite
2 Polite / Not polite
3 Polite / Not polite
4 Polite / Not polite

WRITING

A **Complete the table with sentences from the box.**

What's your email? The room is awesome! My city is beautiful! Where is the hotel?

Question marks	Exclamation marks
______________	______________
______________	______________

B **Complete the sentences with an exclamation mark or a question mark.**

1 How much is it_____
2 No problem_____
3 Thank you_____
4 Where is the coffee shop_____

UNIT 3 Life and Work

LESSON 1 Jobs

VOCABULARY

A 3.1 **Listen and write the words from the box in the correct categories. Then listen and repeat.**

chef doctor lawyer manager pilot teacher waiter waitress

One syllable: ______________________

Two syllables: ______________________

Three syllables: ______________________

B Complete the job descriptions with words from the box.

chef doctor lawyer manager pilot police officer teacher waiter/waitress

1 A ______________ helps people with problems.
2 A ______________ understands the law and rules.
3 A ______________ carries food to people.
4 A ______________ controls a store, a restaurant, etc.
5 A ______________ makes food for people.
6 A ______________ flies to different countries.
7 A ______________ teaches a subject to students.
8 A ______________ gives medicine to sick people.

READING

A Look at the picture. What is the job? ______________

B Read the text quickly and circle the jobs.

My name's Gabriel. I live with my mom, my dad, and my sister, Caroline. I'm a student. I go to college in my town.

My sister goes to college with me. Her major is law. She's also a teacher! She teaches French to people. The lessons are in their homes.

My parents are from France. My mom's a police officer. She isn't a lawyer. She loves her job. My dad is a chef. He works in a hotel. He doesn't like his job.

SKILLS

Practice "scanning" for information: read very quickly and find pieces of information, e.g., jobs, names, etc.

C Read and complete the sentences.

1 ______________ and ______________ go to college in their hometown.
2 Gabriel is a ______________.
3 ______________ teaches French. Her major is ______________.
4 Gabriel's parents are from ______________.
5 Gabriel's mother is a ______________.
6 Gabriel's father is a ______________.

GRAMMAR

A Choose the correct words to complete the rules.

1 We use simple present to **make a general statement** / **ask about the past**.
2 The word order is **different** / **the same** for affirmative and negative sentences.
3 For negative sentences with *I/You/We/They*, we use **don't** / **doesn't** before the verb.
4 For negative sentences with *He/She/It*, we use **don't** / **doesn't** before the verb.

B Unscramble and write the sentences.

1 college / He / to / by / car. / goes ______________________________
2 doesn't / four / She / languages. / speak ______________________________
3 He / a restaurant. / works / in ______________________________
4 work / don't / I / in / a school. ______________________________
5 an apartment. / lives / in / She ______________________________

C Rewrite the sentences correctly.

1 My brother walk to college. ______________________________
2 I loves the city. ______________________________
3 She doesn't goes by bus. ______________________________
4 She don't speak two languages. ______________________________
5 We works in a store. ______________________________

D Complete the sentences using the correct form of the verbs in parentheses.

1 "I'm a teacher. I teach music." He's a teacher. He ______________ (teach) music.
2 "I don't work in an office." He ______________ (not work) in an office.
3 "I live in Lima." Tom ______________ (live) in Lima.
4 "I go to college by train." He ______________ (go) to college by train.
5 "I speak two languages." He ______________ (speak) two languages.

E 3.2 Listen to Sara and complete the description.

Sara's a student. She **1** ___*studies*___ languages. She **2** ______________ English, French, and Spanish. She **3** ______________ Chinese. She **4** ______________ a job. She **5** ______________ in Lima. She **6** ______________ with her parents and her grandfather. Her brother **7** ______________ in Lima. He **8** ______________ in the UK.

VOCABULARY

A Complete the table with words and phrases from the box.

10:00 a.m.   2:00 p.m.   Monday   the afternoon   the evening   the morning   the weekend   Thursday

at	in	on

B Complete the sentences with the correct prepositions.

1 I go to college ____________ the morning.
2 The store is closed ____________ Monday.
3 He starts work ____________ 8:00 p.m.
4 My mom studies ____________ the evening.
5 They work ____________ the weekend.

LISTENING

A 3.3 Listen to the conversation. Where is Linda? Choose the correct picture.

1

2

B 3.3 Listen to the conversation and choose the correct words.

1 The speakers are friends / co-workers.
2 Linda is at work / college.
3 Elly is a student / waitress.

SKILLS

We do not always need to understand every word or every sentence. We sometimes need to listen for pieces of information—e.g., single words (*Saturday*) or numbers (*2:00 p.m.*).

C 3.3 Listen to the conversation and read the summary. Correct the false information.

Linda is a student and a waitress. She works in the coffee shop on Tuesday. She works at the store on Thursday. Her last class finishes at 6:00 p.m. She goes to work by bus. She finishes work at about 8:00 p.m.

GRAMMAR

A Choose the correct answers.

1 What is the correct word order for *yes/no* questions with simple present?

a *Do/Does*—subject—infinitive

b subject—*Do/Does*—infinitive

2 What is the correct word order for *yes/no* short answers?

a *Yes/No*—*do/does/don't/doesn't*—subject

b *Yes/No*—subject—*do/does/don't/doesn't*

B Unscramble and write the questions.

1 you / work / Do / Friday? / on

____

2 store / open / the / Does / in / evening? / the

____

3 on / he / college / go / Wednesday? / Does / to

____

4 8:00 a.m.? / work / Does / at / start / she

____

5 drive / to / Do / the / they / office?

____

C Choose the correct option to complete each sentence.

1 ____________ you go to work by bus?

a Do b Does

2 ____________ the college open on the weekend?

a Do b Does

3 ____________ your sister work in the city?

a Do b Does

4 ____________ your parents come from Mexico?

a Do b Does

5 ____________ he speak two languages?

a Do b Does

D Match the answers to the questions in B. Then complete the answers.

a ______ No, she ____________.

b ______ No, he ____________.

c ______ Yes, I ____________.

d ______ Yes, they ____________.

e ______ Yes, it ____________.

E Read and complete the conversation.

FS: Welcome to Freddie's Stores! This is the online help. My name's Georgia. What's your question?

My name's Katy. **1** ____________ the store open on Sunday?

FS: No, it **2** ____________. Sorry. It opens Monday through Saturday.

3 ____________ the workers speak English?

FS: Yes, they **4** ____________. Our workers speak English, Spanish, French, and Chinese.

5 ____________ the store sell laptops?

FS: Yes, it **6** ____________. The store sells laptops and cell phones.

Thank you for your help.

FS: No problem. Have a great day!

VOCABULARY

A Choose the incorrect item in each group.

1 drink tea / coffee / breakfast
2 eat lunch / table / a sandwich
3 get up bed / early / at 10:00 a.m.
4 go to work / a shower / college
5 take a bath / tea / a shower

B Complete the sentences.

1 I ____________ a bath on the weekend.
2 He ____________ work at 5:00 p.m.
3 They ____________ lunch in the restaurant.
4 My friend ____________ three cups of coffee for breakfast.
5 Do you ____________ early?

READING

A Read the texts and write the correct type from the box. There is one extra type you do not need.

email | job advertisement | online article

1 ____________
____

2 ____________
____

Join Jay's today!

Are you a chef? Do you want a new job at Jay's restaurant?

The restaurant is downtown. It is a popular restaurant. It is very big. The food is always delicious. It's open seven days a week. It opens at 6:00 a.m. and it usually closes at 11:30 p.m. It is sometimes open all night!

Join Jay's today! Complete the application form on our website.

New Message

To: Theo **Cc** **Bcc**

Subject: Lunch on Wednesday?

Hi Theo,
Thanks for your email. Let's meet at Number Ten. I often eat breakfast there. It's a small coffee shop. There are only four tables! I sometimes eat lunch there, but I usually eat lunch at work. How about 12:30 p.m.? Check the website. Do you like it?
Suzie xx

SKILLS

Look at a new text and ask *Who is the reader of the text?* (a friend or a customer?) and *What is the purpose of the text?* (to sell something or to give information?).

B Read the texts in A again and choose *True* or *False*. Rewrite the false sentences correctly.

1 Jay's is a small restaurant. True / False ____________
2 Jay's is open every day. True / False ____________
3 Jay's always closes at 11:30 p.m. True / False ____________
4 Suzie likes Number Ten. True / False ____________

GRAMMAR

A Choose the correct words to complete the rules.

1 We use adverbs of frequency to talk about **where** / **how often** we do something.
2 We put the adverb **before** / **after** the verb *to be*.
3 We put the adverb **before** / **after** other verbs.

B Write the adverbs from the box in order from 0% to 100%.

always never often rarely sometimes usually

C Rewrite the sentences with the adverbs in parentheses.

1 I go to bed early. (always) ______
2 The coffee shop opens on Sundays. (never) ______
3 Do you go to bed early? (usually) ______
4 They eat at home. (rarely) ______
5 There are problems with the food. (sometimes) ______
6 We go to college by bus. (often) ______

D Choose the correct adverbs to complete the sentences.

1 My brother gets up at 6:00 a.m. every day. He **always** / **sometimes** gets up early.
2 I **sometimes** / **never** drink tea. I don't like it.
3 They **rarely** / **often** study in the morning. They go to work in the afternoon.
4 The bus is **sometimes** / **usually** late. It is late one or two days in the week.
5 We **usually** / **never** eat breakfast together at home. We don't eat together on Saturday.
6 The store is **often** / **rarely** closed. I think it's open every day!

E 3.4 Listen and complete the description with the correct adverbs and verbs.

Sammy *always gets up* at 7:00 a.m. She **1** ______ breakfast. She **2** ______ coffee or tea.

Sammy **3** ______ to work by bus. She **4** ______ her car. She starts work at 8:00 a.m. She's a doctor. She finishes work at 9:00 p.m. She **5** ______ late. She loves her job.

Go to p. 125 for Progress Check.

Language and Life

Communication: Meet Someone

FUNCTIONAL LANGUAGE

A **3.5 Listen and complete the conversation.**

Beth: Hey Amber, how are you?

Amber: I'm **1** ____________. And you?

Beth: OK, thanks. Are you free on **2** ____________? Let's go to the park.

Amber: No, sorry. I work on the **3** ____________. How about **4** ____________? I don't work in the **5** ____________.

Beth: Great. Let's go on Friday. How about **6** ____________?

Amber: OK. See you!

Beth: Bye!

B **3.6 Listen and underline the stressed words. Listen and repeat.**

1 Let's go to the park.
2 Let's go on Friday.

WRITING

A **Match the phrases to make sentences.**

1 He works on Saturday, ____
2 I study law, and ____
3 She works in the afternoon ____
4 I usually get up at 7:00 a.m. ____

a and eat breakfast.
b but not in the evening.
c but he doesn't work on Sunday.
d I work in a coffee shop.

B **Check (✓) the correct sentences. Rewrite the incorrect sentences.**

1 ☐ They eat lunch at 12:30 p.m., and they sometimes eat lunch at 2:00 p.m.

____

2 ☐ Let's go to the mall and see a movie.

____

3 ☐ The coffee shop is quiet, but it's very small.

____

4 ☐ They study in the evening but on the weekend.

____

UNIT 4 My City

LESSON 1 Places

READING

A Read the text. What type of text is it? ______________

advertisement article blog

1 ______________________

____

Visitors learn about the history of the city, such as transportation, buildings, and stores.

There is a coffee shop, a restaurant, and a store. There is also a classroom. The classroom is for our teachers to give lectures to schools or colleges.

2 ______________________

____

It opens at 9:00 a.m. and closes at 6:00 p.m. every day. It closes at 4:00 p.m. on Wednesday and Sunday.

3 ______________________

____

The tour starts at the ticket office. (Please buy your tickets before the tour.*) The tour guide shows visitors special parts of the museum. The parts are not open to other visitors. The tour also includes free coffee in the coffee shop.

4 ______________________

____

The tickets cost $20 for adults and $8 for children and students. The museum is free on Mondays.

*The tour costs an extra $15.

B Read the text in A again and complete the text with questions from the box. There is one extra question you do not need.

How much do tickets cost? What do visitors do in the museum? What does the manager do? When does the museum open? Where does the museum tour start?

SKILLS

We do not always need to understand the details. Try reading quickly to find important and useful information.

C Read the text and complete the notes.

Eat at the coffee shop or the **1** ______________

Buy things at the **2** ______________

Learn more in the classroom

Opens at: 9:00 a.m.

Closes at: **3** ______________ */ 4:00 p.m. on Wednesday and* **4** ______________

Tickets: **5** ______________ */ $8 for children and* **6** ______________ *(***7** ______________ *on Monday!)*

tour costs an extra* **8 ______________

VOCABULARY

A Unscramble and write the words.

1 oktsoroeb ______
2 tleoh ______
3 MAT ______
4 akrp ______
5 ummseu ______
6 ispaothl ______
7 trsaarteun ______
8 sbu ntasoit ______
9 foefce hpos ______
10 nsivyurite ______

B Complete the phrases with verbs from the box. Then match to the places in A.

buy eat get learn

1 ______ a bus, a degree, help, money ______
2 ______ a book, a drink ______
3 ______ dinner ______
4 ______ about the past ______

GRAMMAR

A Choose the correct words to complete the rules about simple present information questions.

1 We always / sometimes use a question word at the start of the question.
2 We always / sometimes use *do/does* in the question.
3 We use the word order Question word—subject—*do/does*—verb / Question word—*do/does*—subject—verb.

B Complete the questions with words from the box.

How much What When Where

1 ______ much does a ticket cost?
2 ______ does the store close?
3 ______ do the tours go?
4 ______ does the store sell?

C Match the phrases to make questions.

1 Where do you ____
2 What do students ____
3 How much does a course ____
4 When do you ____
5 What does your family ____

a get to work?
b cost?
c do on the weekend?
d go in the evening?
e learn at college?

D Complete the questions with *do* or *does*.

1 Where ______ people get coffee?
2 When ______ the restaurant close?
3 How much ______ a bus ticket cost?
4 What ______ your parents think about your job?
5 How much ______ students pay for a ticket?
6 When ______ vacation start?

E 4.1 Write the questions for the answers. Then listen and check.

1 ______ teach?
At the new sports center. The big sports center by the train station.
2 ______ teach?
Fitness classes, swimming … I teach everything! The fitness class is always fun. Come and try a class!
3 ______ start?
The class starts at 7:00 p.m. It's on Monday and Thursday.
4 ______ work?
I start work at 10:00 a.m.
5 ______ cost?
The class is $10 for students.

LISTENING

A 4.2 **Listen to the conversation. Where does the woman want to go?**

____

B 4.2 **Listen to the directions. Check the pictures that are correct. Rewrite the directions that are incorrect.**

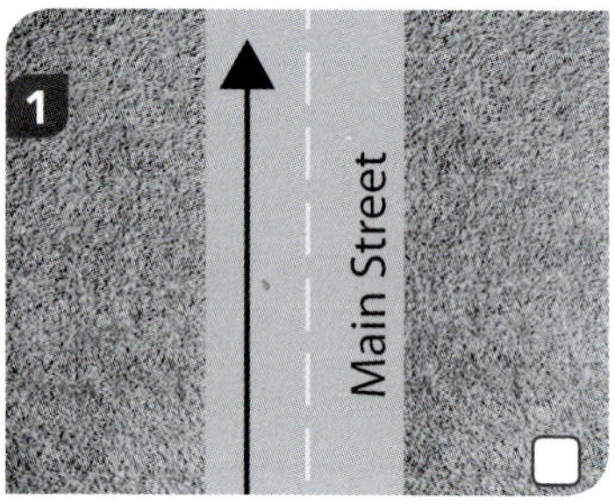

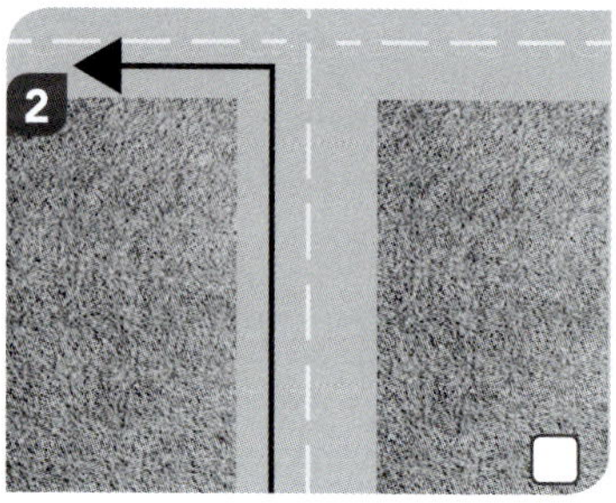

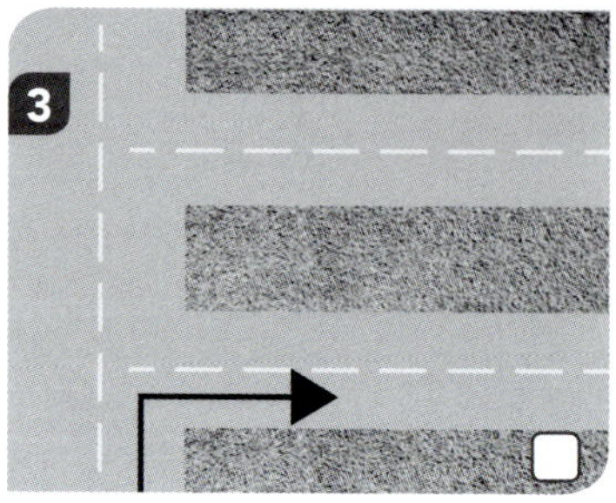

______________________ ______________________ ______________________

______________________ ______________________ ______________________

SKILLS

Key words are words and phrases with the most important information, e.g., *Take the second left. It's on the right.* Underline the key words in these sentences: *Turn left. Take the first right.*

C 4.2 **Listen to the conversation and complete the final directions.**

There's a big ______________________________. The train station is ______________________________.

VOCABULARY

A Match the phrases to make sentences.

1 It's on ______
2 It's on ______
3 The store is across ______
4 My place is between ______
5 The hotel's on ______
6 The college is next ______
7 The ATM is ______

a to the bus station.
b the corner of Fifth Avenue and Tenth Street.
c Top Street.
d on the left.
e from the park.
f the big store and the restaurant.
g the right.

B Complete the sentences.

1 The coffee shop is ____________ the left. It's ____________ the movie theater and the park.
2 I'm on the ____________ of Madison and Riverside.
3 The museum is ____________ Main Street. It's on ____________ right. It's ____________ to the big hotel.
4 Is your new apartment ____________ from the bus station?

GRAMMAR

A Match the phrases to make rules.

1 We use imperatives to ______
2 We do not use a subject ______
3 We use imperatives at ______

a in sentences with directions.
b the start of a sentence.
c give directions and instructions.

B Unscramble and write the sentences.

1 straight / this / up / street. / Go

____

2 and the / the / It's / store / restaurant. / between

____

3 the / where / me, / Excuse / bookstore? / is

____

4 take / and / left / the / right. / second / Turn

____

5 coffee shop / Main. / the / is / and / on / of / Fourth / The / corner

____

6 is / the / from / ATM / college. / across / The

____

C Choose the correct function.

1 It's across from the bookstore. — a asking for directions — b finishing directions
2 Take the first left. — a giving directions — b asking for directions
3 Where's the park? — a giving directions — b asking for directions
4 Excuse me, is the museum near here? — a finishing directions — b asking for directions

D Complete the sentences.

1 A: ______ me, is there an ATM ______ here?
B: Yes, it's on the ______ of Main and Tenth.
2 A: ______'s the Grand Hotel?
B: ______ straight up this road. ______ left. It's on ______ right.
3 A: Excuse ______, where's the language school?
B: ______ right. ______ the second left. It's across ______ the park.

E Read and correct the errors.

WELCOME TO THE CITY!

You are at the train station. Where do you want to go?

City park

Go straight up the road. Take left. Turn the second right. The park is on right.

National Museum

Turn right. Turn the first left. The museum between is the big store and the parking lot.

Shopping mall

Take the #101 bus. The bus stop is across to the train station. The trip is about 10 minutes.

LISTENING

A 4.3 Listen to two conversations. Circle the clothes you hear. There are two extra words you do not need.

bag boots dress jeans pants shirt shoes skirt suit

SKILLS

Listen and focus on important information. The important words are usually nouns, adjectives, or numbers.

B 4.3 Listen to two conversations and complete the sentences.

Conversation 1

1 The skirt is long and ______________. It's $______________.
2 The ______________ are $20.
3 The speakers do not like the ______________ bag.

Conversation 2

4 The man thinks the dress is ______________.
5 The color of the shirt is ______________ or purple.
6 The shirt is dressy and ______________—it's $200.

VOCABULARY

A Complete the words with the correct letters.

1 b______ ______ts
2 dr______ss
3 j______ck______t
4 j______ ______ns
5 p______nts
6 sh______ ______s
7 sk______rt
8 s______ ______t

B Write clothes from the box with the correct parts of the body.

boots dress jacket jeans pants shoes skirt suit

1

2

3

4

1 *jeans* ______________ ______________
2 ______________
3 ______________ ______________
4 ______________ ______________

C Complete the sentences with the correct opposite adjective.

1 The pants aren't dressy. They're ______________.
2 These shoes are very ______________. They're not expensive.
3 I like loose jeans. I don't like ______________ jeans.
4 It's a long skirt. It isn't ______________.

GRAMMAR

A Complete the rules with *this*, *that*, *these*, and *those*.

1 We use ______________ and ______________ for singular nouns.
2 We use ______________ and ______________ for plural nouns.
3 We use ______________ and ______________ for objects very near to us.
4 We use ______________ and ______________ for objects not very near to us.

B **Write the clothes from the box in the correct group.**

boots ~~dress~~ jacket jeans pants shoes skirt suit T-shirt

1 *this/that*: *dress* ______________________________

2 *these/those*: ______________________________

C **Choose the correct words.**

1 I don't like that / those casual suit!

2 Look at this / these shoes!

3 I like that / those jacket.

4 That / Those boots are expensive.

5 This / These skirt is very short.

D **Complete the responses.**

1 A: Those jeans by the door are very expensive. B: Yes, but ____________ jeans here are cheap.

2 A: Do you like this skirt? B: No. I like ____________ skirt by the main door.

3 A: Look at that man! Look at his green shoes! B: ____________ shoes are horrible!

4 A: Is this the suit you want? B: No, I want ____________ suit in the other store.

5 A: These pants are casual. B: Maybe. ____________ pants in the window are dressy.

6 A: That jacket in the window is casual. B: What about ____________ jacket here? It's the same color as my bag! Look!

E **Read and complete.**

Search for people, places and things

Bella's • 9,333 like this

December 18 at 5:40 pm

Hi everyone! Welcome to Bella's fashion blog—live! How are you all?

Look at my great outfit. Look at **1** ____________ red jeans! Aren't they great? Then there's **2** ____________ loose T-shirt and **3** ____________ casual jacket. I love **4** ____________ clothes. Do you like them? Buy **5** ____________ clothes on my website now. There's a special offer today—50% discount!

OK, post your questions below.

Like • Comment • Share

What color is **6** ____________ jacket?

Like • Reply • December 18 at 5:45 pm via mobile

It's brown. It's beautiful!

Like • Reply • December 18 at 5:49 pm via mobile

Are **7** ____________ jeans expensive?

Like • Reply • December 18 at 6:01 pm via mobile

No! They're $40. Today there's a special offer. They are $20 today!

Like • Reply • December 18 at 6:30 pm via mobile

Is **8** ____________ T-shirt dressy or casual?

Like • Reply • December 18 at 6:45 pm via mobile

It's casual. Do you like it? Maybe it's dressy with a skirt?

Like • Reply • December 18 at 7:10 pm via mobile

Go to p. 126 for Progress Check.

Language and Life

Communication: Shop

FUNCTIONAL LANGUAGE

A **4.4 Listen and write the price.**

1

____

2

____

3

________ each

B **4.5 Listen and complete the conversation with words from the box.**

cheap Excuse Here much please take

Buyer: **1** ________ me, how **2** ________ are the books on this table?
Seller: They're $2 each.
Buyer: They're **3** ________! Could I **4** ________ these four books, please?
Seller: Sure. That's $8, **5** ________.
Buyer: Thanks. **6** ________ you are.

WRITING

A **Unscramble and write the adjectives.**

1 ufiletabu ________ jewelry
2 dol ________ book
3 rmeodn ________ apartment
4 sterngietni ________ book
5 almls ________ coffee shop
6 xpievsene ________ clothes
7 uybs ________ store
8 ephca ________ shoes

B **Find the errors and rewrite the sentences correctly.**

1 This is an intersting book.

____

2 Those shoes are cheep!

____

3 It's a apartment modern.

____

4 This shop sells expensive cloths.

____

UNIT 5

Free Time

LESSON 1 Activities

VOCABULARY

A Complete the phrases with words from the box.

bake dance do draw drive play ride (x2) swim

1 ____________ a car
2 ____________ a cake
3 ____________ karate
4 ____________ an instrument
5 ____________ salsa
6 ____________ 1500 m
7 ____________ a horse
8 ____________ pictures
9 ____________ a motorcycle

B Write the correct activity from A for each picture.

1 
____

2 
____

3 
____

4 
____

5 
____

C 5.1 Listen and check (✓) the activities that you hear.

1 ☐ drive a car
2 ☐ bake a cake
3 ☐ swim 1500 m
4 ☐ ride a motorcycle
5 ☐ do karate
6 ☐ play an instrument
7 ☐ draw pictures
8 ☐ dance salsa

LISTENING

A 5.2 Listen to the conversation. Choose *True* or *False*.

1 The speakers are friends. True / False
2 The speakers talk about an ad. True / False
3 The speakers are at a sports event. True / False

SKILLS

Practice listening for "the main idea" = listen for the most important ideas, e.g., the subject of a conversation or the reason the speakers are discussing something.

B 5.2 Listen again and complete the sentences with *Abbie* or *Manuel*.

1 ____________ loves horses.
2 ____________'s sister can ride a horse.
3 ____________ can dance salsa, but ____________ can't.
4 ____________ can play the piano but can't draw pictures.

GRAMMAR

A Complete the rules with words from the box.

questions short answers statements things

1 We use *can/can't* to talk about _______________ we are able / not able to do.
2 For _______________, we use the word order *Can*—pronoun—infinitive.
3 For _______________, we use the word order Pronoun—*can/can't*—infinitive.
4 For _______________, we use the word order *Yes/No*—pronoun—*can/can't*.

B Unscramble and write the questions and answers.

1 drive / you / Can / Yes, / can. / car? / a / I
____

2 they / the / Can / play / guitar? / can't. / No, / they
____

3 ride / Can / Yes, / she / can. / a / she / motorcycle?
____

4 bake / mom / she / Can / cake? / can't. / your / a / No,
____

5 can. / he / Yes, / Can / karate? / he / do
____

C Complete the answers.

1 Can she draw? No, _______________.
2 Can you ride a horse? Yes, _______________.
3 Can they drive a car? No, _______________.
4 Can he draw pictures? Yes, _______________.
5 Can they play an instrument? Yes, _______________.
6 Can your dad dance salsa? No, _______________.

D Match the phrases to make sentences.

1 I can dance salsa, _____
2 I can ride a horse, but _____
3 I can't play the guitar, _____
4 I can draw pictures, and _____
5 I can speak English, _____
6 I can bake a cake, _____

a I can't ride a motorbike.
b but I can't understand Chinese.
c I can write stories.
d and I can cook pasta.
e but I can play the piano.
f and I can sing.

E Read the conversation and correct the errors.

A: What do you do?
B: I'm a teacher. I teach karate.
A: Wow! I can't play karate. Can you do other sports?
B: Yes. I can swim, but I can ride a horse. I love music, but I can dance salsa. Can you dance salsa?
A: No, I can. My brother is a dancer. He studies at a dance school. He can dance, but he can sing. He's amazing!
B: What do you do? Are you a student?
A: No, I'm a chef.
B: So you can dance, but you can cook delicious meals.
A: Yes, I can't!

VOCABULARY

A Write the name of the subject or the thing.

1 

a________

2 

m________

3 

m________

4 

p________
b________

5 

s________
g________

6 

c________

B 5.3 Listen and write the name of the subject or the thing.

1 dictionary **3** ________ **5** ________ **7** ________
2 ________ **4** ________ **6** ________

READING

A Read and write the type of text from the box. ________

ad for a college magazine article online profile

What do you study?

Art and languages. I speak three languages. **1** ________ is my first language. My other languages are English and Chinese. My friend's mom is from **2** ________. We speak Chinese together. It's fun!

What's your favorite subject?

Art! I love it! I draw every day. I can draw pictures, and I can draw **3** ________. My sister is an artist. I sometimes use my sister's **4** ________. They're great.

Nestor Gonzalez @NestorF
Followers

What's your daily routine?

I get up early. I usually get up at 6:00 a.m. I **5** ________ in the morning. Then I go to college. I drive my dad's **6** ________. It's old but it's OK. I finish college at about 5:00 p.m. I drive to the sports center or meet friends. I always eat dinner with my family, and I go to bed about 10:00 p.m.

What are your favorite things?

I love this **7** ________. It's very useful. It's my mom's. She's a teacher. I also like my new **8** ________. They're for my dance class. They're black and beautiful.

B Complete the sentences in A with words from the box. There are two extra words you do not need.

car cartoons China dictionary draw guitar music paint brushes shoes Spanish

C Read the text in A and complete the sentences.

1 Nestor speaks three languages. He speaks ____________ with his friend's mom.
2 Nestor's favorite subject is art. His sister is an ____________.
3 Nestor draws in the morning and then he goes to ____________.
4 Nestor's favorite things are his mom's ____________ and his shoes. The shoes are for his ____________ class.

SKILLS

Key words are the important words in a sentence. These words help us to understand the main idea and the details. For example:
~~The~~ course starts ~~in~~ September.
Cross out the words that are not key words:
The class finishes at 7:00 p.m.

GRAMMAR

A Choose the correct words to complete the rules.

1 We use the possessive *'s* for **things we own or people we are connected to** / **things and people from our country**.
2 We use *'s* after a **name or noun** / **verb or adverb**.
3 The possessive *'s* **means** / **doesn't mean** the same as a contraction.

B Circle the possessive *–s*.

My friend's brother is a teacher. His name is Tommy and he teaches music. I go to his music class on the weekend. Tommy's classes are very popular. I play the piano and I sometimes play my friend's guitar.

C Find the errors and rewrite the words adding the possessive *–s*.

1 Is this your bag? No, it's Emily bag. ____________
2 Where's your father car? It's over there. ____________
3 My teacher name is Mr. Smith. He's over there. ____________
4 Who is Amanda dad? The man next to the door. ____________
5 When is the college new website live? Tomorrow. ____________

D Use the prompts to write sentences.

1 car—my sister
This is my sister's car.
2 books—Jon
____
3 phone—my friend
____
4 calculator—Colin
____
5 paint brushes—the teacher
____

E 5.4 Listen and write the sentences.

1 *Are these Pablo's shoes?*
2 ____________
3 ____________
4 ____________
5 ____________
6 ____________

VOCABULARY

A Write the correct word from the box under each picture. There is one extra word you do not need.

cloudy rainy snowy sunny windy

1 

2 

3 

4 

______ ______ ______ ______

B Choose the correct sound for the underlined vowels.

1	cool	a /iː/	b /uː/
2	cloudy	a /ɑʊ/	b /eʊ/
3	freezing	a /ɪ/	b /iː/
4	hot	a /ɒ/	b /ʌ/
5	rainy	a /eɪ/	b /eʊ/
6	snowy	a /ɒ/	b /eʊ/
7	sunny	a /ʌ/	b /ɒ/
8	windy	a /ɪ/	b /eɪ/

LISTENING

A 5.5 Listen to three voicemails and choose the correct option.

1 Jason isn't in the office / is in the park / isn't in the café.
2 Diana isn't in the office / is in the park / isn't in the café.
3 Lulu isn't in the office / is in the park / isn't in the café.

B 5.5 Listen to the voicemails again and match the person to the reason.

1 Jason's having coffee ______
2 Diana isn't working in the office ______
3 Lulu's walking ______

a because there's a problem in the building.
b because the weather is freezing.
c because there are no cabs.

SKILLS

To understand more about the speaker and the situation, listen for why the speaker is doing something. For example, *I'm having dinner with my family because it's my birthday.*

C 5.5 Listen to the voicemails again. Choose *True* or *False*. Rewrite the false sentences correctly.

1 Jason is talking to Angelica. True / False
______
2 Jason's brother is wearing his new jeans. True / False
______
3 Diana is changing one or two parts in the report. True / False
______
4 Diana isn't very busy today. True / False
______
5 Lulu is looking for Kim. True / False
______
6 Lulu is playing soccer in the park. True / False
______

GRAMMAR

A Match the phrases to make rules.

1 We use the present progressive to ____
2 We use *to be* ____
3 We add *–ing* to ____
4 We use different spelling ____

a the end of the main verb.
b for irregular verbs.
c before the main verb.
d talk about activities that are happening now.

B Complete the sentences with the correct form of *be*.

1 I'm ____ (+) watching TV.
2 We ____ (–) eating dinner.
3 He ____ (–) shopping at the mall.
4 You ____ (+) playing the guitar.
5 They ____ (+) speaking Chinese.
6 She ____ (–) sleeping in her bed.

C Complete the sentences.

1 He's reading ____ (read) a book.
2 They ____ (not do) their homework.
3 She ____ (not watch) a movie.
4 The girls ____ (get) coffee.
5 It's ____ (rain) today.
6 I ____ (not have) fun.

D Write sentences using the present progressive.

1 They / swim / in the ocean. ____
2 She / not study / at college. ____
3 I / not / ride a motorcycle. ____
4 He / play / the piano. ____
5 You / not eat / your lunch. ____

E Read the online post. Correct the five errors.

What are you all doing?

Hey! What's up? Here we are at home. We're busy students because we studying to be doctors! We arent studying tonight. We're relaxing. Sean's eat pizza. Navid talking on his phone. Karen's sleepping now! What are you all doing?

____
____
____
____
____

Go to p. 126 for Progress Check.

Language and Life

Communication: Your City

FUNCTIONAL LANGUAGE

A Match the phrases to make sentences.

1 **Don't go** in ____ a a cup of coffee.
2 **Eat** ____ b the morning.
3 **Get** ____ c at BB's restaurant.
4 **Go** ____ d the museum.
5 **Visit** ____ e to the city park.

B Complete the sentences with the bold imperatives in A.

1 ______________ the museum. It's very interesting. ______________ at the pizza restaurant across from the museum. It's awesome! ______________ on Monday. It's very busy and there are no free tables.

2 ______________ to the beach. ______________ a sandwich at the beach café. ______________ to the beach restaurant, because the waiters aren't friendly.

WRITING

A Choose the correct word.

1 Do you like coffee **and** / **because** / **or** tea? I drink five cups of coffee every day.
2 Reserve a table, **and** / **because** / **or** the restaurant is very busy.
3 Go to the museum **and** / **because** / **or** go to the park. They're both great!

B Complete the sentences with *and*, *or*, or *because*.

1 We go on Sunday ______________ it's free.
2 Tourists usually get a tour bus ______________ see the city.
3 The restaurant isn't open in the morning ______________ on Monday.

UNIT 6 Health

LESSON 1 Appearance

VOCABULARY

A Complete the sentences with the correct word.

1 I have blue eyes and big e________. My nose isn't small, but my m________ is small. I have good t________.
2 He's tall and h________. He has big arms and big l________. He has b________ hair.
3 They have d________ hair. They aren't t________. They're short and s________.
4 You are t________ and slim. You have brown e________ and d________ hair.
5 My dad has g________ hair. He's s________ and heavy. He has bl________ eyes.

B Write the words from the box in the correct category.

arm blond ears eyes gray leg mouth nose short slim tall

Color	Face	Body
dark	*teeth*	*heavy*

C 6.1 Listen and match the underlined vowels (1–7) to the sound (a–g).

1 /e/
2 /oʊ/
3 /ɑʊ/
4 /ɑr/
5 /iː/
6 /eɪ/
7 /ai/

a gray ____
b teeth ____
c eyes ____
d mouth ____
e nose, old ____
f dark, arm ____
g heavy, leg ____

LISTENING

A 6.2 Listen and write *Francesca* and *Sebastian* next to the correct picture.

1
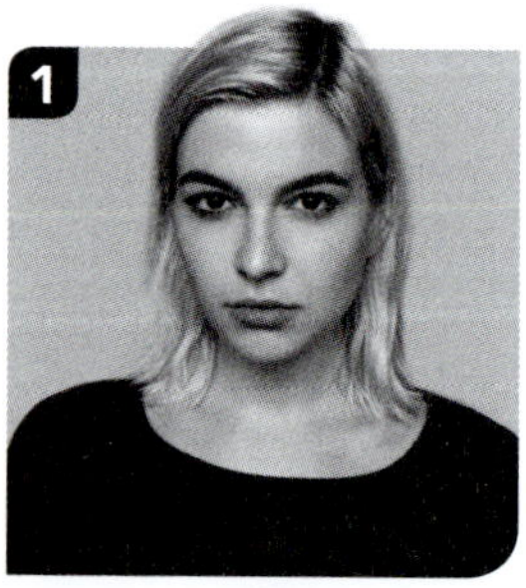
____

2

____

3

____

4
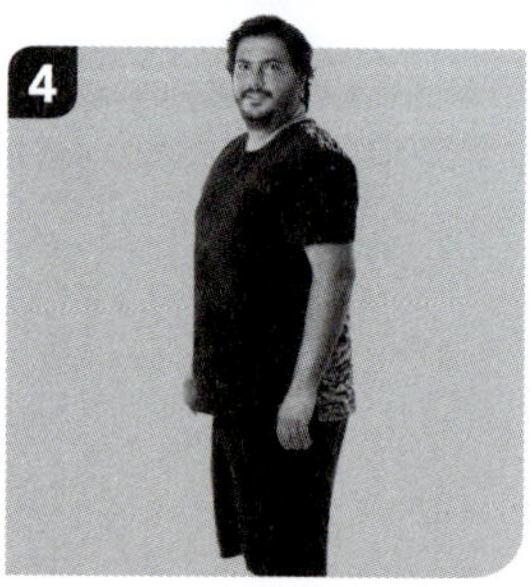
____

B 6.3 **Listen to the conversations and complete the descriptions.**

Dwayne

Body: short and **1** ____________

Face: **2** ____________ hair and a big **3** ____________

Dan

Face: **4** ____________ hair and big **5** ____________

Body: tall and **6** ____________

SKILLS

Practice listening carefully for the information you need. This helps you to learn the difference between information that is important and information that is not important.

GRAMMAR

A Match the phrases to make rules.

1. We use *have* to describe ____
2. We use *have* with ____
3. We use *has* with ____
4. For negative statements, we use ____

a *I/You/We/They*.

b *don't* or *doesn't* before *have*.

c a person's face and body.

d *He/She*.

B Complete the sentences.

1. He ____*has*____ (+) dark hair and green eyes.
2. You ____________ (–) brown hair. Your hair is blond.
3. She ____________ (–) a big nose.
4. I ____________ (+) big ears and a big mouth.
5. We ____________ (–) big eyes. We have small eyes.
6. She ____________ (+) dark hair and brown eyes.

C Choose the correct option.

1. She **don't** / **doesn't** have dark hair.
2. The brothers **has** / **have** brown hair and blue eyes.
3. She **is** / **has** short and slim.
4. He **has** / **have** blond hair and green eyes.
5. My parents **are** / **have** tall and heavy.
6. They **don't** / **doesn't** have blue eyes.

D Rewrite the sentences correctly.

1. He's brown eyes and brown hair. ____________
2. They have tall and heavy. ____________
3. I doesn't have gray hair. ____________
4. She have a very big nose. ____________
5. Fiona has young and beautiful. ____________

E Read and complete the descriptions with the correct verb.

Jack **1** ____________ tall and slim. He **2** ____________ blond hair. His sister **3** ____________ dark hair. They both **4** ____________ green eyes. Jack's parents **5** ____________ short and slim.

I **6** ____________ long, dark hair and brown eyes. I **7** ____________ blue eyes. I don't like my ears because they're big. I **8** ____________ small ears. My dad **9** ____________ small ears and gray hair. He **10** ____________ short and heavy.

VOCABULARY

A Read the clues and complete the crossword.

Across

2 Eat an … on toast or use one to bake a cake.

5 Add milk and eat for breakfast.

7 A cold meal that is usually green.

8 You usually eat this for lunch.

Down

1 These are hot and they are usually green. They are part of a meal.

3 A type of white meat.

4 An animal from the ocean.

6 A cold drink.

B 6.4 Listen and write the words in the box in the correct group.

cereal chicken coffee eggs fish juice pasta salad sandwich tea toast vegetables

One syllable	Two syllables	Three syllables
eggs, ___	___	___
___	___	___

READING

A Read and identify the type of text.

advertisement social media page story

Search for people, places and things

The Green Room

Good morning! It's a sunny day in the city. Our chefs are making lunch for our busy customers. There's some pasta, some salad, and some sandwiches. What's your favorite meal and why? Tell us and win a meal for four people at our restaurant.

Lindy
Good morning! My favorite meal is breakfast. I start work at 11:00 a.m., so I have a big breakfast. I eat hot cereal, toast, and some fruit. I love coffee. ♥ I have three big cups of coffee for breakfast! It's my favorite meal because the house is usually very quiet.
Like • Reply • December 18 at 6:09pm via mobile

Ralph
Hello! My favorite meal is dinner because my mom makes delicious meals. I usually eat dinner with my parents and my sister. My mom often cooks fish or pasta. She makes fresh juices, and she bakes cakes. ☺ I watch my mom make meals because I want to be a chef.
Like • Reply • December 18 at 6:09pm via mobile

SKILLS

What types of text do you read in your first language? Do you read advertisements, blogs, stories, online articles, or another type? Look at a new text in English and read the text quickly—what type of text is it?

B Read and complete the sentences.

1 The weather is ______________.
2 The chefs at the restaurant are making ______________.
3 The restaurant has a competition for ______________ people to win a meal.
4 Lindy eats a big breakfast and drinks three big ______________ of coffee.
5 Lindy likes this meal because her home is usually ______________ in the morning.
6 Ralph ______________ eats dinner with his parents and his sister on Sunday.
7 Ralph watches his mom cook because he wants to be a ______________.

C Complete the sentence with information that is true for you.

My favorite meal is ______________ because ______________________________.

GRAMMAR

A Choose the correct option to complete the rules.

1 We use *some* and *any* to talk about the
 a size of different things. **b** number of different things.
2 For negative statements and questions, we use
 a any. **b** some.
3 For affirmative statements, we use
 a any. **b** some.

B Choose the correct word.

1 There are any / some eggs on the table.
2 They don't have any / some time to make breakfast.
3 There is a / an sandwich for lunch.
4 Sorry, there isn't any / some coffee.
5 I have a / an apple every morning.
6 There are any / some delicious vegetarian meals.

C 6.5 Listen and complete the conversations.

1 A: Let's have ______________ cup of tea.
 B: Oh, no, I don't like tea. Do you have ______________ coffee?
 A: No, sorry. Would you like ______________ orange juice?
 B: OK, thanks.
2 A: Is there ______________ pasta?
 B: Yes, there is. There is ______________ fish and there are ______________ vegetables, too.
 A: OK. Is there ______________ bread?
 B: No, there isn't.
3 A: Do you want ______________ cereal for breakfast?
 B: No, thanks.
 A: How about ______________ egg and ______________ toast?
 B: Yeah. Thanks.

LESSON 3 Feelings

VOCABULARY

A Write the words.

1 /bord/ ___bored___
2 /'hʌngri/ __________
3 /'taiɚd/ __________
4 /ɛk'saitɪd/ __________
5 /sæd/ __________
6 /hæpi/ __________

B Complete the sentences.

1 I'm __________. I want to sleep.
2 Are there any sandwiches? I'm very __________.
3 He's __________ because his friends are on vacation.
4 Are you __________ about our vacation? I am!
5 She's __________ because she doesn't have a job.
6 Laura is __________ about her new job.

LISTENING

A 6.6 Listen to the introduction and choose the correct option.

1 It is a **radio show** / **street survey**.
2 There is a short interview with a **person from the city** / **famous chef**.

SKILLS

The first part of an interview or lecture has important information. It has information about the main idea, the other ideas, the people, and other interesting points.

B 6.7 Listen to the rest of the interview and number the information in the correct order.

a ______ Mina's family
b ______ Mina's favorite place to eat
c ______ Mina's favorite stores
d ______ Mina's job
e ______ when Mina cooks

C 6.7 Listen to the interview again and complete the sentences.

1 Mina's family is from __________.
2 Mina teaches __________ and __________ to children.
3 The school is __________ the park and __________ the old museum.
4 Mina can play the __________, but she can't __________.
5 Mina __________ makes a big meal __________.
6 Mina's husband __________ cooks __________.
7 Mina's favorite store sells old shoes, jackets, and __________ and the prices are __________.
8 The manager of The Full English is from __________, and Mina teaches his __________.
9 Steve has __________ hair and a big __________.
10 Mina gives Tony some food for lunch: __________ salad with some pasta, __________ juice, and __________ cake.

GRAMMAR

A Complete the descriptions with the correct grammar points from the box.

adverbs of frequency   *can*   prepositions of place   present progressive   *to be*

1 We use ______________________ to describe someone's ability.
2 We use ______________________ to explain where something is.
3 We use ______________________ to make very simple statements about our life.
4 We use ______________________ to say how often we do something.
5 We use ______________________ to say what we are doing now.

B Unscramble and write the sentences.

1 the / man / Is / your / grandfather? / tall

____

2 in / two / There / museums / city. / are / the

____

3 but / They / speak / can't / French, / English. / speak / they / can

____

4 the restaurant / ATM / The / between / the / shop. / is / coffee / and

____

5 at / He / up / 5:30 a.m. / gets / always

____

6 there / some / eggs. / pasta, / some / There's / are / and

____

C Match the sentence or question (1–6) to the grammar type (a–f). Use the bold words to help you.

1 **When does** the store **open**? ____
2 There are **two phones** and **three notebooks** in my bag. ____
3 They study **on the weekend**. ____
4 My **friend's bag** is under the bed. ____
5 **We're eating** a snack. ____
6 **Does** the manager **come** from Spain? **Yes, he does.** ____

a *yes/no* questions with simple present
b possessive *'s*
c present progressive
d simple present information questions
e prepositions of time
f plural nouns

D Circle and correct one error in each sentence.

1 We're from Mexico. We lives in Mexico.
2 I start usually work at 8:00 a.m.
3 We watching a movie because it's cold and rainy.
4 He can ride a horse, but he cann't ride a motorcycle.
5 Do your sister go to college?

E Read and complete the profile.

1 __________ morning, my name's Caroline. **2** __________ from France. I'm French, and **3** __________ first language is French. I speak English **4** __________ Chinese. I'm **5** __________ lawyer, and I work in New York City. I live with my husband and our son, Pierre. Pierre **6** __________ to college. He **7** __________ music and art. He **8** __________ play three or four musical instruments. He usually plays soccer on the **9** __________. He **10** __________ sleeping right now.

Go to p. 126 for Progress Check.

Language and Life

Communication: Café

FUNCTIONAL LANGUAGE

A Match the phrases to make sentences and questions.

1 What can I ____
2 Can I ____
3 What size: ____
4 Any other ____
5 Is that coffee ____
6 Can I get ____
7 That's $4.50, ____
8 Here's your ____

a drinks?
b you some food?
c for here or to go?
d please.
e get you?
f change.
g small, medium, or large?
h get a coffee, please?

B 6.8 Listen and complete the waiter's notes.

Drinks: ____________
____
Where: ____________
____
Food: ____________
____
Total: ____________
____
Change: ____________
____

WRITING

A Write the type of error from the box is in each sentence.

capital letter | punctuation | spelling | word order | wrong word

1 I like Coffee. ____________
2 The food is delicious, and the waiters aren't friendly. ____________
3 Do you like tea ____________
4 One black coffe, please. ____________
5 This is a restaurant busy. ____________

B Rewrite the sentences from A correctly.

1 ____________
2 ____________
3 ____________
4 ____________
5 ____________

Progress Check

UNIT 1 — PAGE 88

Lesson 1

- ☐ I can learn about greetings. *Review? Go to VOCABULARY/ LISTENING, p. 6*
- ☐ I can introduce myself. *Review? Go to GRAMMAR, p. 7*

Lesson 2

- ☐ I can talk about countries and nationalities. *Review? Go to READING/VOCABULARY, p. 8*
- ☐ I can give personal information. *Review? Go to GRAMMAR, p. 9*

Lesson 3

- ☐ I can talk about family members. *Review? Go to VOCABULARY/LISTENING, p. 10*
- ☐ I can describe my family. *Review? Go to GRAMMAR, p. 11*

UNIT 2 — PAGE 95

Lesson 1

- ☐ I can describe places. *Review? Go to VOCABULARY/LISTENING, p. 16*
- ☐ I can introduce my partner. *Review? Go to GRAMMAR, p. 17*

Lesson 2

- ☐ I can talk about my things. *Review? Go to VOCABULARY, p. 18 and GRAMMAR, p. 19*

Lesson 3

- ☐ I can describe where things are. *Review? Go to VOCABULARY, p. 20 and GRAMMAR, p. 21*

UNIT 3 — PAGE 102

Lesson 1

- ☐ I can talk about jobs. *Review? Go to VOCABULARY/READING, p. 26*
- ☐ I can describe my partner. *Review? Go to GRAMMAR, p. 27*

Lesson 2

- ☐ I can talk about time and work. *Review? Go to VOCABULARY, p. 28 and GRAMMAR, p. 29*

Lesson 3

- ☐ I can talk about daily activities. *Review? Go to VOCABULARY, p. 30*
- ☐ I can describe my daily routine. *Review? Go to GRAMMAR, p. 31*

UNIT 4 — PAGE 109

Lesson 1
- [ ] I can talk about places in a city. *Review? Go to VOCABULARY, p. 36*
- [ ] I can talk about a tour. *Review? Go to READING, p. 37*

Lesson 2
- [ ] I can give and ask for directions. *Review? Go to VOCABULARY, p. 38*
- [ ] I can describe where places are. *Review? Go to GRAMMAR, p. 39*

Lesson 3
- [ ] I can talk about clothes. *Review? Go to VOCABULARY, p. 40 and GRAMMAR, p. 41*

UNIT 5 — PAGE 116

Lesson 1
- [ ] I can talk about free-time activities. *Review? Go to VOCABULARY, p. 46*
- [ ] I can talk about what I can/can't do. *Review? Go to GRAMMAR, p. 47*

Lesson 2
- [ ] I can learn about subjects. *Review? Go to VOCABULARY/READING, p. 48*

Lesson 3
- [ ] I can talk about types of weather. *Review? Go to VOCABULARY, p. 50*
- [ ] I can describe what people are doing. *Review? Go to GRAMMAR, p. 51*

UNIT 6 — PAGE 123

Lesson 1
I can talk about appearance. *Review? Go to VOCABULARY, p. 56*
I can describe people's appearances. *Review? Go to GRAMMAR, p. 56*

Lesson 2
I can talk about food and meals. *Review? Go to VOCABULARY, p. 58 and GRAMMAR, p. 59*

Lesson 3
I can talk about feelings. *Review? Go to VOCABULARY, p. 60*

Notes

Macmillan Education
4 Crinan Street
London N1 9XW
A division of Macmillan Education Limited

Companies and representatives throughout the world

Speak Your Mind Starter Level Student's Book + Workbook
ISBN 978-1-380-03090-0
Speak Your Mind Starter Level Student's Book + Workbook + access to Student's App and Digital Workbook ISBN 978-1-380-03665-0
Speak Your Mind Starter Level Student's Book + Workbook + access to Student's App ISBN 978-1-380-03666-7

Written by Rhona Snelling

The author has asserted her right to be identified as the author of this work in accordance with the Copyright, Designs and Patents Act 1988.

First published 2020

Designed by QBS Learning
Illustrated by Jerome Brasseur/Beehive Illustration pp. 16(t), 57(r); Daniel Deamo/Lemonade Illustration pp. 16(b), 68, 69; Bunky Hurter/Mendola Artists p. 28(b), p. 67; Zhen Liu/Shannon Associates p. 56, Keith Favazza/Wendy Lynn & Co. pp. 4, 34, 57(l), 65, 69; Lon Eric Craven/Wendy Lynn & Co.; QBS Learning pp. 4, 20, 28(t), 38, 42, 50, 54, 63, 66, 79, 90, 102, 104, 106(t), Greg Paprocki; Martina Farrow.
Original cover design by therestless.co.uk
Cover adaptation by Roberto Martinez
Cover photographs by **Getty Images**/Chatuporn Sornlampoo/EyeEm (background), Getty Images/Morsa Images (upper body), Getty Images/Westend61 (lower body); **Shutterstock**/279photo Studio (window).
Picture research by Fernanda Rocha (Ikonia LLC) and Emily Taylor

Authors' acknowledgements
Rhona would like to thank the wonderful editorial team at Macmillan Education for their enthusiasm and positivity during the development of this course. She hopes that the course will be beneficial and enjoyable to teachers and students alike. She would also like to thank her lovely family and friends for their kind support.

The publishers would like to thank all the teachers that piloted and reviewed the series, and a special thanks to Annette Flavel for content and cultural reviews.

The authors and publishers would like to thank the following for permission to reproduce their photographs:
Student's Book: **Alamy Stock Photo**/Cultura Creative (RF) p. 6(1), Alamy Stock Photo/Tzogia Kappatou p. 62(1), Alamy Stock Photo/Oksana Korniyenko p. 67(5), Alamy Stock Photo/Dmitrii Melnikov p. 45, Alamy Stock Photo/Panther Media GmbH p. 58(2, bc); **Getty Images** pp. 10(br), 18(5), 26(6), 28(br), 50(inset), 43, Getty Images/Aminart p. 46(4), Getty Images/Asia Images p. 48(4), Getty Images/Chaiyaporn Baokaew p. 10(1), Getty Images/Blend Images p. 36(7), Getty Images/bubaone p. 10(icons), Getty Images/Michael Cogliantry p. 50(tcl), Getty Images/Creative Crop p. 18(3), Getty Images/Cultura RM Exclusive/yellowdog p. 26(7), Getty Images/Dan Dalton p. 40(bc), Getty Images/DigitalVision Vectors/Leontura p. 8(1-flag, 2-flag), Getty Images/Dorling Kindersley p. 18(2), Getty Images/E+/chinaface p. 30(2), Getty Images/E+/FotografiaBasica p. 67(3), Getty Images/iStockphoto pp. 7, 12(cr), 30(cr), 41, Getty Images/E+/JohnnyGreig p. 36(9), Getty Images/E+/Juanmonino p. 48(Brad's mother), Getty Images/E+/kate_sept2004 p. 46(5), Getty Images/E+/kirin_photo p. 58(1), Getty Images/E+/MediaProduction p. 46(6), Getty Images/E+/petekarici p. 36(br), Getty Images/E+/RichLegg p. 26(8), Getty Images/E+/swetta p. 36(6), Getty Images/Shannon Fagan p. 30(1), Getty Images/Foxys_forest_manufacture p. 30(3), Getty Images/Mitchell Funk p. 36(2), Getty Images/Globe Turner, LLC p. 8(3, 4), Getty Images/Glowimages p. 36(1), Getty Images/Hero Images pp. 36(10), 48(1), Getty Images/Hill Street Studios LLC p. 48(3), Getty Images/Hinterhaus Productions p. 50(Barney), Getty Images/Julia Hoersch p. 58(4), Getty Images/Image Source p. 36(5), Getty Images/Image Source/Stanton j Stephens p. 46(8), Getty Images/iStockphoto pp. 18(1, 9), 46(8), Getty Images/jackSTAR p. 40(bl), Getty Images/Jetta Productions p. 26(1), Getty Images/Christopher Kimmel p. 40(5), Getty Images/Lonely Planet/Neil Setchfield pp. 36(4), 38, Getty Images/Lonely Planet Images/Diego Lezama p. 62(2), Getty Images/Davide Marzotto/EyeEm p. 50(tr), Getty Images/Diana Miller p. 58(6), Getty Images/Mint Images p. 36(8), Getty Images/Peter Muller p. 48(7), Getty Images/Ippei Naoi p. 52, Getty Images/Taiyou Nomachi p. 48(5), Getty Images/Dimitri Otis p. 40(2), Getty Images/pbombaert p. 18(4), Getty Images/petekarici p. 18(10), Getty Images/Portra p. 10(2), Getty Images/Rubberball p. 32, Getty Images/Rubberball/Nicole Hill p. 18(cr), Getty Images/Leslie-Ann Smith/EyeEm p. 48(br), Getty Images/Sol de Zuasnabar Brebbia p. 46(2), Getty Images/Chatuporn Sornlampoo/EyeEm pp. 5, 15, 25, 35, 45, 55 (top and bottom banner) - 6, 8, 10, 14, 16, 18, 20, 24, 26, 28, 30, 34, 36, 38, 40, 44, 46, 48, 50, 54, 56, 58, 60, 64(top banner), Getty Images/Alexander Spatari pp. 26(bl), 58(br), Getty Images/Nehru Sulejmanovski/EyeEm p. 67(2), Getty Images/swetta p. 12(1), Getty Images/Tetra Images p. 30(5), Getty Images/twomeows p. 30(4), Getty Images/UpperCut Images p. 26(3), Getty Images/Dougal Waters pp. 10(3), 46(1), Getty Images/Westend61 pp. 40(4), 26(4), 58(5), Getty Images/William Whitehurst p. 36(3), Getty Images/YinYang p. 33(c); **Image Source**/Allen and Kleantho p. 26(2); **iStockphoto**/gpointstudio p. 26(5), iStockphoto/Dean Mitchell p. 46(3); **Shutterstock/Aerodim** p. 26(br), Shutterstock/Africa Studio p. 40(3), Shutterstock/AJR_photo pp. 13, 48(Brad), Shutterstock/Belish p. 67(6), Shutterstock/Daxiao Productions p. 44, Shutterstock/ESB Professional p. 33(t), Shutterstock/Iconic Bestiary p. 15(icons), Shutterstock/Jaroslav Francisko p. 58(3), Shutterstock/Gorodenkoff p. 48(6), Shutterstock/Graphical_Bank p. 12(2), Shutterstock/Harbucks p. 8(Jane), Shutterstock/Jiri Hera p. 5, Shutterstock/John Roman Images p. 33(b), Shutterstock/krsmanovic p. 22, Shutterstock/Svetlana Larina p. 30(br), Shutterstock/RUBEN M RAMOS pp. 65, 66, Shutterstock/matthew25 p. 50(tl), Shutterstock/Dusan Milenkovic p. 50(tcr), Shutterstock/Monkey Business Images p. 6(2), Shutterstock/Sergey Nivens p. 15, Shutterstock/PT Images p. 10(1), Shutterstock/PureSolution p. 35(icons), Shutterstock/Rawpixel.com p. 55, Shutterstock/Rido p. 8(Alberto), Shutterstock/salajean p. 50(tc), Shutterstock/Roman Samborskyi p. 24, Shutterstock/Atiketta Sangasaeng p. 23, Shutterstock/Theeradech Sanin p. 67(4), Shutterstock/Shchus p. 25, Shutterstock/Syda Productions pp. 8(Tino), 35, 48(2), Shutterstock/Taweepat p. 48(bc), Shutterstock/Paisit Teeraphatsakool p. 67(7), Shutterstock/giedre vaitekune p. 12(3), Shutterstock/wavebreakmedia p. 6(3), Shutterstock/Wichaiwish p. 18(6), Shutterstock/Lim Yong Hian p. 48(cm); **Stockbyte** p. 18(7); **Superstock**/Chris Ryan/OJO Images/Exactostock - 1775 p. 46(7); **123RF**/Goran Bogicevic p. 67(1), 123RF/robert hyrons p. 48(cr), 123RF/pixelrobot p. 18(8).

Workbook: **Alamy**/Cultura Creative p. 87(tl), Alamy/Elizabeth Whiting & Associates p. 90(tr); **Getty Images** p. 92(c,f), Getty Images/Aminart p. 111(3), Getty Images/Cecilie Arcurs p. 99(bl), Getty Images/Creative Crop p. 92(g), Getty Images/Cultura RF pp. 96(tr), 124, Getty Images/Digital Vision p. 97(cm), Getty Images/Dorling Kindersley p. 92(b), Getty Images/EyeEm p. 115(4), Getty Images/EyeEm/Leslie-Ann Smith p. 113(4), Getty Images/FG Trade p. 89(tr), Getty Images/fStop p. 118(1), Getty Images/Geber86 p. 100, Getty Images/Hill Street Studios p. 113(2), Getty Images/ImageSource p. 99(br), Getty Images/iStockphoto p. 85(tr, 1), Getty Images/iStockphoto/m-imagephotography p. 118(3), Getty Images/iStockphoto/Mustafagull p. 118(4), Getty Images/Kate_sept2004 p. 111(4), Getty Images/William King p. 97(bl), Getty Images/René Mansi p. 119, Getty Images/Maskot p. 120, Getty Images/MediaProduction p. 111(5), Getty Images/Monkeybusinessimages p. 101, Getty Images/Peter Muller p. 113(3), Getty Images/Oriba p. 90(tl), Getty Images/Pbombaert p. 92(d), Getty Images/Petekarici p. 92(a,j), Getty Images/Ian Ross Pettigrew p. 118(2), Getty Images/Picture Press RM p. 103(tr), Getty Images/Andrew Rowat p. 104, Getty Images/Dougal Waters p. 111(1), Getty Images/Westend61 p. 87(tr); **iStockphoto** p. 111(2); **Scanrail** p. 92(e); **Shutterstock** p. 106, Shutterstock/Africa Studio p. 111(br), Shutterstock/ESB Professional p. 87(family), Shutterstock/Flamingo Images p. 96(br), Shutterstock/Gligatron p. 107(tr), Shutterstock/Volodymyr Goinyk p. 112, Shutterstock/g-stockstudio p. 84, Shutterstock/J. Helgason p. 87(frame), Shutterstock/Arek Malang p. 98, Shutterstock/Petr Malyshev p. 114, Shutterstock/Matthew25 p. 115(1), Shutterstock/Dusan Milenkovic p. 115(3), Shutterstock/Mortazza p. 110, Shutterstock/Sean Pavone p. 90(br), Shutterstock/Photo Melon p. 113(5), Shutterstock/PixieMe p. 113(br), Shutterstock/Pressmaster p. 117(tm), Shutterstock/Marco Rubino p. 117(b), Shutterstock/Salajean p. 115(2), Shutterstock/Ljupco Smokovski p. 116, Shutterstock/Syda Productions p. 113(1), Shutterstock/Paisit Teeraphatsakool p. 113(6), Shutterstock/Rawpixel.com p. 86, Shutterstock/Marco Rubino p. 107(br), Shutterstock/RossHelen p. 123, Shutterstock/YARUNIV Studio p. 122, Shutterstock/Wichaiwish p. 92(i); **Solstock** p. 85(tl); **Macmillan Education Ltd**/Mexico p. 95; **Stockbyte** p. 92(h); **Superstock** p. 85(2,3,4); **Westend61** p. 89(cm).

The author(s) and publishers are grateful for permission to reprint the following copyright material:
"Macmillan English Dictionary Online" © Macmillan Education Limited 2019, Published by Macmillan Education, a division of Macmillan Education Limited. Used by Permission. All Rights Reserved

Printed and bound in Uruguay

2024
37